MEMORY, RELATED FUNCTIONS AND AGE

MEMORY,
RELATED FUNCTIONS
AND AGE

JACK BOTWINICK

and

MARTHA STORANDT

Washington University
St. Louis, Missouri

CHARLES C THOMAS · PUBLISHER
Springfield · Illinois · U.S.A.

Published and Distributed Throughout the World by

CHARLES C THOMAS • PUBLISHER

Bannerstone House

301-327 East Lawrence Avenue, Springfield, Illinois, U.S.A.

© *1974, by* CHARLES C THOMAS • PUBLISHER

ISBN 0-398-03143-6

Library of Congress Catalog Card Number: 74-1495

With THOMAS BOOKS *careful attention is given to all details of
manufacturing and design. It is the Publisher's desire to present books
that are satisfactory as to their physical qualities and artistic possibilities
and appropriate for their particular use.* THOMAS BOOKS *will be
true to those laws of quality that assure a good name and good will.*

Printed in the United States of America

W-2

Library of Congress Cataloging in Publication Data

Botwinick, Jack.

Memory, related functions, and age.

Includes bibliographical references.

1. Memory.   2. Age and intelligence.   I. Storandt,
Martha, joint author.   II. Title. [DNLM: 1. Memory.
2. Memory Disorders—In old age.   BF371 B751m 1974]

BF371.B68   153.1   74-1495

ISBN 0-398-03143-6

PREFACE

MEMORY LOSS IN later life has often been documented by research evidence and has more often been commonly taken for granted as a fact of life. Extreme memory loss is as incapacitating as any major setback; it can reach the proportions of almost complete inability. Extreme memory loss can require almost total custodial care.

Very fortunately, such extreme loss is not the rule; it is the exception. More minor memory problems, however, are not so exceptional—they are found often.

It is surprising, therefore, that so few comprehensive studies have been made on this very important topic. There are many studies in the published literature, each reporting one or two types of memory measurements; there are none that we know that make effort to measure a large variety of types and to determine relationships of these with other important behaviors. There are none we know of that make effort for a more comprehensive understanding of memory ability in later life. This report is of just such an effort.

The investigation was helped in no minor way by the National Institute of Child Health and Human Development (NICHD) of the U.S. Public Health Service. Their training grant (HD-00047) partially supported this effort; the information which was developed here is used in the training of the students.

Our thanks go to the NICHD and also to two people who were especially helpful to us. We thank Mrs. Isabel Gerber, who did everything possible to assist us, from typing manuscripts to keeping track of the many details. We also thank Professor Walter Hudson, Chairman, Department of Social Policy and Practice, School of Social Work of Washington University. He is a top-notch statistician who was always available for statistical advice, answering questions for us as they came up.

To the NICHD, Mrs. Gerber, and Professor Hudson, we gladly acknowledge our appreciation.

JACK BOTWINICK
MARTHA STORANDT

CONTENTS

MEMORY, RELATED FUNCTIONS AND AGE

CHAPTER ONE

SCOPE AND ORGANIZATION
OF THE STUDY

MANY ABILITIES AND functions as they relate to adult age were investigated in this study, but the major focus was memory—many different kinds of memory. The problem of memory in later life is so important that many cognitive, perceptual, and personality dimensions may depend on it. For example, a failing memory may add to self-doubt, it can contribute to feelings of diminishing personal and social control; it can make learning difficult; it can alter the functional environment. The present study is concerned with memory and age, and with such facets of ability and personality that may be related to it.

FOCI OF THE INVESTIGATION

There were six foci of study. 1. The major focus, *memory,* constituted more than half of the data collected. Data bearing on the related foci were collected with procedures which may be categorized into the following: 2. Clinical tests of *brain function* or brain damage, which seem to call for abilities in perception, some involving speed of response. 3. Tests of *psychomotor speed,* and 4. Tests of *intelligence.* Noncognitive functions were also measured, with procedures bearing on 5. *Personality* and *morale;* and on 6. *Health* and *habits.* The health and habits tasks called for impressions or questionnaire responses by both the investigators and the subjects.

Memory/Learning

Popular and scientific opinion seem compatible with respect to the age pattern of memory ability. Wechsler (1961, p. 154) concluded, "Practically all studies, as well as common experiences, testify to its progressive decline in later years." Jones and Kaplan (1956, p. 128), after reviewing literature, wrote, "The fact remains that memory defects are, perhaps, the most salient psychological symptom in aging. . . ."

There does not appear to be any published disagreement with such statements when the word, "memory," is used. There is contention, however, when the word, "learning," is used. Despite this, memory and learning are not easily distinguished; they do not seem to be at all distinguishable operationally. Typically, learning is measured as a change in response from one experience or trial to another, while memory is measured as change in relation to the time between experiences (Melton, 1963, p. 3). The difference is simply whether it is the experiences that are noted, or whether it is the seconds, minutes, or days between experiences that are of concern. Perhaps it would be best to think of memory as "memory/learning."

This may be most apparent when carrying out studies in short-term recall. In a verbal learning study, for example, the experimenter may read a list of words to the subject with the instruction to learn them and to say them out loud. In the saying of them, however, memory is involved. On the other hand, the instruction might have been to memorize the words and to say them out loud. Here, it is apparent, it was necessary to learn the words before they could be memorized. The unity of memory and learning is less apparent when the time between learning experiences is a matter of days or years. By undeclared convention, the function or process is typically called memory when such long-time intervals are involved; with very short-time intervals, they have been called both memory and learning.

There is disagreement as to whether short-term memory and long-term memory are subserved by different mechanisms. This disagreement has been explicated in a variety of sources in the published literature, and it need not be discussed here, except to indicate that the controversy will not be settled until more data, less conflicting than now present, become available. Those who support a one-mechanism view, i.e. that one mechanism explains both short- and long-term recall, do so by pointing to literature showing that the same factors affecting one also affect the other—factors such as repetition and interference. Paradoxically, those supporting a two-mechanism view support it for just the opposite reasons, i.e. factors affecting short-term memory do not always affect long-term memory.

It is difficult to carry out laboratory investigations of long-term memory without bringing to bear many artifacts. Perhaps it is for this reason that there are relatively few studies on long-term memory. In fact, not only is short-term memory more often investigated, but a popular practice is to measure recall only after three to eighteen seconds following the presentation of stimuli (as seen in a comparison of studies by Melton, 1963). Not all studies do this, however; short-term memory has also been studied with a delay of minutes after experiencing the stimuli. The present investigation similarly focuses more on short-term memory than long-term, but the latter is investigated too.

A last distinction needs to be made in regard to memory studies. In some studies recall is measured, in others recognition is the prime interest. Most of the procedures in the present study are of recall—information must be retrieved from a memory store. A few of the procedures, however, are of recognition. It is often held that recognition does not involve retrieval; instead, it involves a matching of information in the memory store with information in the environment. While ability to recall is seen to decline with age, the ability to recognize does not, or does so to a very much smaller degree (e.g. Schonfield, 1965).

All the memory procedures used in this study are experimental procedures developed specifically for the purposes of the present investigation. The procedures of the other functions are, for the most part, tests already described in the research literature. All these procedures will be described in detail later.

Brain Function/Perception

Clinical tests of brain damage are similar in some ways to many experimental laboratory tasks that are difficult for older people. Such comparisons have led to analogies between the processes of adult aging and brain damage. This may make for unfair and dangerous speculation.

> It is to be emphasized that, if there are behavioral similarities between aged individuals and brain-damaged patients and if the same or similar theories or models are useful in both types of investigations, it is not to be assumed that aged brains are damaged or have lesions. All that may be said is that there is an analogy. . . . (Botwinick, 1959, p. 759).

Rather than apply labels such as brain damage, it is preferable to describe specific abilities or processes. For example, Reed and Reitan (1963) administered twenty-nine tests and ranked them on a continuum between those measuring recall of stored information and those of problem-solving relatively unrelated to prior experience. Tests of the latter type had been found difficult for brain-damaged subjects. They have also been found difficult for elderly subjects. It may be concluded from this that a cognitive difficulty for many older people involves problem-solving ability, especially when past experience cannot be brought to bear. Many of these problem-solving tasks require perceptual skills, thus the designation, "brain/function perception."

Psychomotor Speed

There is little doubt that as people age they become slower in responding to environmental events and in carrying out their activities. What this indicates, however, is not certain. For many investigators the available evidence suggests that the central nervous system underlies the slowing, which, if carried to an extreme point, might suggest that the greater the loss of speed in advanced age, the greater the decrement in central nervous system functioning. Speed of response, therefore, becomes an index of intactness of the central nervous system.

This is an extreme position and probably a wrong one because many factors determine how quickly people can respond. Nevertheless, it may be equally wrong to maintain that functioning of the central nervous system is unrelated to speed of responding and of carrying out activities quickly. There is evidence that the central nervous system is related to speed of performance, but the evidence is indirect and very often based upon negative results (see review by Botwinick, 1965).

If the slowing of responses with adult aging is of central origin, it might be expected that the slowness would be related to cognitive and perceptual abilities. The present investigation provides data to test this possibility. Performances on speed tests were examined in relation to those of brain function/ perception, intelligence and others. All of these were examined in relation to the age of the subjects.

A distinction must be made that is frequently overlooked: speed of carrying out an activity and speed in responding to an environmental event are not identical processes; they may not even be related (Botwinick and Storandt, 1973). The present investigation is concerned only with the former speed processes. For a thorough analysis of the relationship between behavioral speed and central nervous system functioning, a recent report may be consulted (Botwinick, 1973, Chapter 12).

Intelligence

Probably no age-related function has been more thoroughly researched than that of intelligence. Still, the available information is not without controversy nor without further need of elucidation, although some very important information has been developed.

It had been said earlier, in discussing brain function, that ability to solve problems that bear little or not at all on past experience seems to decline in later life, but those abilities which are dependent upon stored information and prior achievement hold up well. In essence, this is the major research finding of intelligence in relation to age, at least in terms of research based upon cross-sectional investigations. Recent reports of longitudinal investigations have cast doubt regarding these generalizations, emphasizing instead the maintenance of function in later life. However, it is too early to be sure of this—more longitudinal studies are needed. With cross-sectional investigations, the generalizations have been confirmed many times.

Personality/Morale

In describing personality traits that may change as people age, it sometimes is difficult to evaluate them in proper perspective. Perhaps, it is the relative constancy of personality, more than change, that characterizes aging people. At least one large scale investigation concluded that "personality type was independent of age" (Neugarten, Crotty and Tobin, 1964, p. 187).

One personality characteristic which is evident in many aging adults is that of turning inward; elderly people tend to disengage from activities and from interaction with other people. They do this despite the fact that personal satisfaction and good morale are associated more with activity than with disengagement. However, even though satisfaction and activity tend to go together most of the time, this is not true for all people. Those of good health, those who have high self-regard, and those who are self-directed seem quite content in disengagement (Neugarten, Havighurst and Tobin, 1968).

There appears to be increased conformist and passive patterns in later life (Neugarten and Gutmann, 1958); emotions seem less intense, and achievement needs tend to be diminished. Cautiousness, depression, and hypochondriasis are greater among the aged than among the young (see Botwinick, 1973, Chapter 5).

Health/Habits

Good health, both physical and mental, provides the opportunity for a satisfactory life, irrespective of considerations of activity or disengagement (Maddox and Eisdorfer, 1962). Health status, in fact, underlies much of what else seems important to good morale and positive outlook. For example, Garrity and Klein (1971) studied patients who had very recently suffered heart attacks; they studied these patients during the first five days of their hospitalization. In a most dramatic way, they observed that those patients with much negativism regarding their illnesses or patients whose attitudes became worse in their hospital stay had high mortality rates after discharge. But, upon further analysis, it was seen that those who had these negative attitudes tended to be those who had histories of prior poor health. They were the same patients who had previous heart trouble. Thus, it was seen that health status underlay the attitudes which seemed related to cardiac functioning.

The prescription for good health, especially in later life, seems to be: keep active and exercise; keep food intake low, especially fats; don't smoke cigarettes. This prescription is especially helpful to ward off or minimize cardiovascular diseases, the major killer, by far, of all diseases seen in late life (U.S. PHS report, 1970).

STRATEGY OF ANALYSIS AND ORGANIZATION

Since the scope of the study was wide and there were many measurements, it was thought best to analyze segments of the data separately as well as together. A general overview of the organization may be seen by the following:

1. The various categories of behavior related to memory were analyzed as a group, e.g. brain function/perception, psychomotor speed.

2. The various categories of memory function were analyzed as a group, e.g. long-term memory, short-term memory span.

3. The two sets of data—memory and related functions—were correlated.

4. Steps in the first two sets of analyses above included separate examination of the various categories. Also included was an examination of each of the individual measures.

The program of data analysis above shows that from the individual test scores to progressively larger units of test scores, relationships in regard to age were examined. The individual measures were examined by way of variance analysis. Analyses of grouped measurements included multivariate analysis, corrrelation, and factor analysis. These will be described in more detail in the next chapter.

In summary then, this book tells of a study of a variety of behavioral functions in relation to age, with the major emphasis on memory. Some of the many questions asked in this study are: Given many contexts and types of memory, do they show similar age patterns? Can they be grouped in relatively few dimensions? On what other behavioral functions do they bear? Do these latter functions vary with age? Can these be grouped into relatively few dimensions?

The functions other than memory investigated were categorized in groups designated as: brain function/perception, psychomotor speed, intelligence, personality/morale, and health/habits. Together with memory, study of these functions pointed to new understandings of aging processes.

CHAPTER TWO

TASKS, SUBJECTS AND DATA ANALYSIS

TASKS

MORE THAN FIFTY tasks were used in this investigation. The tasks of memory/learning were developed especially for the present purposes, whereas the tasks of the other functions were standardized or otherwise reported in the literature. There were approximately thirty memory/learning tasks organized into seven groups of procedures and twenty tasks of related functions organized into five groups. Among the latter were four tasks of brain function/perception, three of psychomotor speed, and five were of intelligence. Personality/morale was assessed by four procedures, as was health/habit. Many of these latter, related function tasks were made up of several subtests. Women subjects were tested with all the procedures while men were tested with all the memory/learning ones and only about half of the others.

All the tasks are listed in Appendix A in the order in which they were administered. They will be described in detail later when the results are presented, but the description will not be in the order of test administration. Instead, the description will be in an order designed to provide a clearer view of the investigation. First the data bearing on the various related functions will be presented and in the order indicated above, i.e. beginning with brain function/perception and ending with health/habit. Following this, the memory/learning part of the investigation will be described. The final chapter of the book focuses on the relationships among all these data.

SUBJECTS

Effort was made to recruit people for study of the age decades twenties through the seventies with the goal of having the age groups as homogeneous with respect to their socioeconomic backgrounds as possible. While this goal was not completely met, in many important aspects it was. There were ten men and ten women in each age decade; their age ranges, means, and standard deviations are presented in Table I. It may be seen in this table that the men and women were very similar in age.

TABLE I

AGE (YEARS) OF SUBJECTS IN THE STUDY

Range		Mean		Standard Deviation	
Male	*Female*	*Male*	*Female*	*Male*	*Female*
21-29	22-29	25.3	25.8	2.4	2.9
30-38	30-39	34.0	35.9	2.7	3.2
40-49	40-49	44.8	44.5	3.0	3.3
51-57	52-57	52.6	55.2	2.2	2.0
61-69	60-69	65.0	63.6	2.8	2.4
70-79	70-80	73.6	74.9	3.7	3.0

The 120 men and women were independent, community dwelling volunteers, with all but three from the metropolitan St. Louis area. They were drawn from various sources, including church and community organizations, a local apartment building for retired persons, evening classes at Washington University, friends, neighbors, and acquaintances of the project staff or of other subjects. Although each person served as a subject for from two to five hours of interview and testing, none was paid for his participation in the project. In this regard, they may be unique in the population.

Table II shows the mean education level of this sample by age decades. An analysis of variance of the number of years of education revealed a significant age effect ($F = 10.44$, df $= 5,108$, $p < .0001$) and a significant age by sex interaction ($F = 6.40$, df $= 5,108$, $p < .0001$).

The decline in number of years of formal education with increasing age, in combination with the change in the quality of formal education within the past fifty years, is a common confounding effect in cross-sectional age comparisons. The age pattern in education of the present sample as it compares to national averages may be seen in Figure 1. The 1970 Census

TABLE II

YEARS OF EDUCATION OF THE SUBJECTS OF THE STUDY

Age	Male		Female	
	Mean	*S.D.*	*Mean*	*S.D.*
20-29	14.70	1.49	13.40	2.37
30-39	15.00	0.82	15.40	1.71
40-49	14.30	0.95	13.70	2.71
50-59	15.00	2.40	11.60	1.58
60-69	10.30	3.43	11.80	2.53
70-80	9.22	2.44	13.30	3.68

(their Table 199, 1973) reported median years of schooling by age for white men and women. A comparison of these data and the present ones (Figure 1) indicate that the present sample seems better educated than the Census sample, particularly for ages thirty to forty-nine.

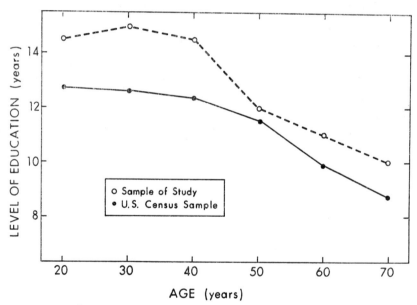

Figure 1. The present sample compared to a national sample reported by the U.S. Census Bureau in median years of formal education. National medians were reported by half decades for men and women separately. These were averaged.

In cross-sectional comparisons, educational differences with age may best be thought of as a cultural or generational effect—a reflection of differences among age groups in opportunities and expectations, rather than a reflection of intrinsic interests or abilities. Therefore, in comparing people of different age, their occupational or role statuses may be more meaningful than education levels as a guide to comparability. With this in mind, the subjects were given a score with respect to occupational level and age comparisons made. The scaling of occupations was made in the manner of Hollingshead (1957), where the head of household determined occupational status. An analysis of variance of the occupation scores failed to disclose statistically significant differences ($p > .05$) in regard to age ($F = 1.49$, $df = 5,103$); sex ($F = 0.26$, $df = 1,103$); or the interaction between age and sex ($F = 0.97$, $df = 5,103$).[1]

The occupations of the sixty men ranged from presidents, executives, and managers of medium or large businesses, through small businessmen, salesmen, and middle managers. One subject was a truck driver, one a machinist, and one a warehouse worker. One man described himself as a "jack-of-all trades" and one was unemployed at the time of testing. The bulk of the men in this sample gained their livelihood from occupations relating to the business world; the professions were represented by two engineers, one elementary school principal, and a counselor to hospital patients and their families. Fifteen of the men were retired; they were all in their sixties and seventies. Approximately one-third of the women in the sample were housewives, with the remainder of the sample representing primarily clerical occupations; there were several teachers, a punch press operator, a registered nurse, a home economist, and a medical technologist.

------

[1]Men subjects, when considered apart from women, were statistically different in their occupational statuses in relation to age ($p < .01$), but women were not ($p > .05$). Since in the present study no analysis of test performance is of men alone but many analyses are of women alone, the analysis of occupational status of both men and women points to the adequacy of age group matching.

Hollingshead (1957) combines occupational status and education level in an index of socioeconomic status. This index, however, is so much a function of education level that it was thought more useful for the present purpose to keep occupation and education separate.

Five of these women, all in their sixties and seventies, described themselves as retired.

Of the 120 people comprising this sample, ninety-five were married at the time of testing. Fifteen were single, four were divorced, and six were widowed.

DATA ANALYSIS AND PRESENTATION

When the performances of people of different ages are compared and found different statistically, explanations accounting for the finding must include considerations both of age or maturational effects and of cultural or cohort effects (e.g. Schaie, 1967). This simply reflects the fact that older people were born and raised in different eras than younger people; thus their cognitive stimulation and opportunities, their expectations and values, may have been different. This makes interpretation of cross-sectional studies difficult.

It was indicated that in the present study the age pattern in the level of education was similar in some ways to the age pattern nationally, i.e. less formal education with increasing age. It was also indicated that the occupational levels of the subjects in this study were similar among the age groups. One implication of this is that generalizations may be made from the present subject sample to a much larger population of similar socioeconomic level, but the generalization must be made recognizing the confounding effects of age and education, i.e. cohort differences. It would be ideal if it were possible to conclude that an observed age difference is attributable more to maturational effects than to educational or cultural ones, but, unfortunately, this is not possible in cross-sectional studies such as the present one.

An effort was made to minimize variable cultural effects so that the observed age differences might be seen as having a greater basis in a maturational change. Cultural effects were minimized first by sampling, i.e. by selecting subjects as homogeneous in regard to their socioeconomic (occupational) levels as possible. Second, accepting the age differences in educational levels of the subjects as an index of cultural effects, a type of variance analysis was carried out which permitted an examination of age effects as statistically free as possible from the confounding influences of education. This analysis is described as item No. 2 below.

The overall plan and pattern of data analysis is described next in specific and technical detail. Readers who are not interested in these details can skip them and proceed to the next chapter.

1. When several procedures were thought of as constituting a unitary category (e.g. brain function/perception), with each procedure measuring an aspect of a larger function, a multivariate analysis of variance was carried out to determine whether the six age groups were different overall.[2] The multivariate analyses were carried out in the manner of Bock (1963, 1966) and Bock and Haggard (1968). Only general summaries indicating probability levels will be reported of this type of analysis.

When, however, the several procedures within the category were thought of as levels of variations of the same function, a within-subject design analysis of variance was carried out. This analysis, as well as the multivariate analysis, included the ordering of independent variables described next.

2. To minimize the effects of educational factors among the subjects of different age, a step-down, least-squares analysis of variance was reported for each test measurement. This analysis (Overall and Spiegel, 1969) permits the ordering of effects such that those analyzed later in a sequence are adjusted for by those analyzed earlier. For example, in the present study, education differences and then, when possible, sex differences were ordered first (in the nonorthogonal hierarchical design). Thus, when age effects were examined, the results were already adjusted for or took into account the fact that education and sex differences

---

[2]In the multivariate analysis, all interactions except that between age and sex were pooled and tested against the within-groups variance estimate. When the pooled interaction was found not significant ($p > .05$), it was combined with the within-groups variance to form a residual variance. This residual variance served as the error term for tests of significance of the three main effects, i.e., age, sex, and education, and of the age-by-sex interaction. When, however, the pooled interaction was found to be a statistically significant source of variation, each of the interaction terms was tested using the within-groups variance estimate as the error term.

might underlie some of the differences in performances otherwise attributed to age. In other words, a statistically significant age difference when these adjustments are made may be taken as a conservative estimate of the effect of the age of the subjects on their test performances.[3] In the present study, the influence of education was analyzed in terms of whether the subject had twelve or more years of formal schooling or had less than twelve.

3. When age differences were found statistically significant in the hierarchical analysis, a further statistic was used to determine how important age was in the test performances. The percent of variation in test scores that could be attributed to age, as adjusted for education and sex effects, was determined by omega square (ω^2) in the manner described by Hays (1963, p. 406-407). Thus, both information of statistical significance and of the extent that age accounted for the performances were determined.

4. When age differences were not found statistically significant ($p > .05$) in the step-down analysis, the data were reanalyzed ordering age first and education last in the nonorthogonal hierarchical design. With regard to age, this is comparable to the more traditional analysis of variance where age differences are confounded with education and sex differences. In the interpretation of the results, cultural or cohort influences would be given greater emphasis when age is found statistically significant only when ordered first in the step-down analysis (and not when it is ordered last).

5. The nonorthogonal step-down analysis provided estimated mean performance scores for each age decade, i.e. least squares estimates of the means accounting for unequal subclass size. These were reported in tables. In addition, the observed means, those computed on the basis of the actual scores made by individual subjects, were shown in figures. (The estimated means and the observed means are the same in orthogonal analyses.)

6. Both the memory data and the data of the related func-

---

[3]Whatever the sources of variation of the error terms used in the multivariate analysis, they were used also in the univariate analyses. It should be recalled that only those effects reaching significance in the multivariate analysis may be appropriately interpreted in terms of the respective individual analyses of variance.

tions were reduced, each by principal component analysis. There were two analyses with the related function data and one with the memory data. Two were carried out in the former instance because men were not tested with all procedures. One analysis was of the scores of women subjects alone, the other analysis of men and women combined. The principal component analysis of the memory data was of both men and women subjects.

7. The final analysis included principal component solutions of the memory and related functions together.

In summary, then, two techniques, sampling and statistics, were used in an effort to minimize the cultural effects which are intertwined with the maturational effects. It should be emphasized that the cultural effects were not eliminated by these techniques; they were only minimized. In a relative sense, therefore, maturational effects were maximized.

Part I

BRAIN FUNCTION, PERSONALITY, HEALTH AND OTHER FUNCTIONS

CHAPTER THREE

BRAIN FUNCTION/PERCEPTION

IT WAS SAID EARLIER that tests discussed in this chapter largely measure perceptual abilities and were developed for the main purpose of examining known or suspected brain damage. The concept "brain damage" suggests either a presence or an absence of the damage, with its presence described in extent and locus of lesion. The concept, brain function, on the other hand, suggests only level; it does not imply presence versus absence of damage. It is brain function that is the concern here—it is conceived simply as a continuum of a behavioral ability.

Four tasks constitute the brain function battery. Three of these are more or less standard clinical tests and one is a procedure that has often been used in the experimental literature. The clinical tasks are The Hooper Visual Organization Test (from here on called the VOT), and the Trailmaking tests, both parts A and B. The fourth test is an experimental one, the Embedded Figures Task.

PROCEDURES

VOT

Hooper's (1958) test is of thirty drawings of simple objects. These drawings are of black lines on white paper background with no shading and no dimensional realism. Each of the thirty drawings is segmented into parts which are rearranged into a type of jigsaw puzzle. The subject tries to spatially organize or integrate the parts so that they become, in mind, a unified, recognizable picture drawing. The job is to name the drawings, even if it is just a guess. Although there is no time limit, the subject is told to work as quickly as possible.

The reliability of the test has been reported as 0.82 with college students as subjects and 0.78 with neurotic patients in a state hospital. Correlations between age of the subject and VOT test scores were found statistically not significant with hospital mental patients but statistically significant with residents from a home for the aged ($r = -0.57$). "This is interpreted as reflecting the influence on the test scores of the normal aging processes in the brain" (Hooper, 1958, p. 5).

Trailmaking

This test is in two parts, A and B. It was first developed for the U.S. Army in 1944 and has had wide but relatively unstandardized usage since then. Part A of the test comprises twenty-five numbered circles that are spread out in an apparent random order on a standard size sheet of typewriting paper. The subject is first given a sample sheet of eight such circles with the instructions: "Begin at Number 1 . . . and draw a line from 1 to 2 (the experimenter pointing), 2 to 3 . . . and so on, in order, until you reach the end. . . . Draw lines as fast as you can." Following this the subject is given the test proper of twenty-five circles to connect by pencil.

Part B of the test also comprises twenty-five circles, but only thirteen are numbered, the other twelve enclose letters of the alphabet (A through L). This test is also given with a sample accompanying the instructions. They are to draw a line from 1 to A, A to 2, 2 to B, B to 3, and so on until L to 13.

In performing the parts A and B, errors are called to the subject's attention, and the subject is requested to correct them. However, errors are not scored except indirectly: the score on both parts A and B is the time it takes to complete the task; errors take time to point out and correct and are thus involved in the scoring. To keep all performance scores of the present study in the same direction, i.e. to have all good performances scored with high numbers and poor performances with low numbers, the reciprocal of time was used as the score. This reciprocal was multiplied by 1000 to do away with decimals.

Embedded Figures

This task has been administered in various forms and under a variety of names, e.g. embedded figures, concealed figures, Gottschaldt's figures, and combinations of these. In each of the forms, the task is to find a geometric pattern which is embedded in a more complex mesh of other patterns. An example of a simple task may be to find a cross of a certain size and type in a complex of horizontal and vertical lines. Tasks of this type differentiate between brain damaged and control subjects (e.g. Battersby, et al., 1953), and there is evidence that they may differentiate between types of brain lesions. For example, subjects with posterior lesions were seen to perform more poorly than subjects with anterior lesions (Teuber, et al., 1951).

The test battery of the present study was the one used by Thurstone (1944). Each subject was first presented with two example problems. In the first, the figure to be found was shown along side of the complex in which it was embedded. Part of the complex was drawn with dark lines to outline the figure so that it was easily seen. In the second example, the figure and complex was also presented side by side, but the subject had to darken the lines to show the figure clearly.

After this, each subject was given a five-part series of embedded figures tasks. In the first part, twenty-seven tasks were given on the same page, each similar in type to the second example. Part 2 had only seven tasks, all on one page; the same figure was to be found in each of seven different complexes. This task was made more difficult by the fact that the figure was placed on top of the page and the complexes beneath it. There were also seven tasks in part 3, but with these, one of two figures had to be found in each complex. As in part 2, the figures were presented on the top of the page. Parts 4 and 5 were similar to part 3, except there were ten complexes in each part and the figures were more difficult to find.

In a general way, the five parts were meant to represent different levels of test difficulty. On each of the five parts, the score was of the percentage correct, permitting comparisons in performance among the five parts.

RESULTS

The performance scores on the VOT and Trailmaking tests (A and B) were included in a multivariate analysis of variance[1] comparing men and women, age groups, and education levels. The embedded figures test scores were omitted from the multivariate analysis because only women were examined with this task. The multivariate analysis of the VOT and Trailmaking performances showed statistically significant effects ($p < .0001$) for each of the three main sources of variation, i.e. age, sex, and education; the interaction between age and sex was not significant ($p > .05$). The statistically significant results of this multivariate analysis permitted univariate analyses of the VOT and Trailmaking data. The nature of the significant differences and the statistical analyses of the embedded figures data are described next.

VOT

A summary of the univariate analysis of the performance scores on Hooper's Test of Visual Organization is shown in Table III. In this analysis the age effect was adjusted for differences in test scores that are associated with the subject's sex and

TABLE III

ANALYSES OF VARIANCES OF SCORES ON THREE
BRAIN FUNCTION/PERCEPTION TESTS

		Tests		
Source	*df*	*VOT*	*Trail A*	*Trail B*
Educ. (E)	1	49.08†	20.67†	12.07‡
Sex (S)	1	26.35†	0.03	0.95
Age (A)	5	11.70†	3.97§	3.74§
A X S	5	0.58	1.06	0.83
Residual*	107	(13.78)	(132.41)	(32.60)
Total	119			

* Residuals are represented by mean squares. All other sources of variation are represented by F-ratios.
† $p < .0001$
‡ $p < .001$
§ $p < .01$

[1]See Chapter 2, section on Data Analysis and Presentation.

education level, i.e. whether or not the subject had more than twelve years of formal schooling.[1] This analysis indicated that the six age groups were significantly different in regard to their performances of visual organization ($p < .0001$). Table IV (estimated means accounting for unequal subclass size) and Figure 2 (observed means) show the nature of these differences.

TABLE IV

BRAIN FUNCTION/PERCEPTION: ESTIMATED
PERFORMANCE MEANS BY AGE DECADES

Tests	*Age (Years)*					
	20s	*30s*	*40s*	*50s*	*60s*	*70s*
VOT (No. correct)	26.56	24.30	25.06	22.22	22.19	17.79
Trail A (1/sec)*	37.07	36.67	30.42	30.93	26.21	22.13
Trail B (1/sec)*	18.07	17.12	15.42	14.99	12.62	11.06
Emb. Fig. (% correct)	73.14	57.55	76.14	74.59	38.73	43.84

* The reciprocal of seconds was multiplied by 1,000 to eliminate decimals in the recording and analysis of the data.

Increasing age was associated with decreasing performance. An ω^2 analysis showed that 22 percent of the test score variance was accounted for by age. When only the scores of women subjects were analyzed, ω^2 was .28.

Sex differences were also observed, with women performing better than men ($p < .0001$). The age decline, however, was not different for one sex from the other (the interaction between age and sex was not statistically significant, $p > .05$). Those subjects with more than twelve years of formal education performed better than those with less ($p < .0001$), but no interaction involving education was statistically significant ($p > .05$).

Trailmaking

Table III shows that the age groups differed in their performance on both parts A and B ($p < .01$), with age accounting for 10 percent of the test score variance (ω^2) on each. The

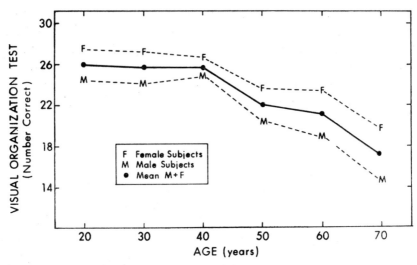

Figure 2.   Mean Hooper Test of Visual Organization score as a function of age.

observed mean scores for men and women were plotted in Figure 3 to demonstrate the similarity of their age patterns— the interaction between age and sex was not statistically significant ($p > .05$). Unlike the results of the variance analysis based upon the VOT scores, statistically significant sex differences were not found with either the Part A or Part B Trailmaking scores ($p > .05$). Again, however, education differences were significant ($p < .001$), with those with more than twelve years of education performing better than those with fewer years of formal education. Estimated means may be seen in Table IV.

In addition to separate analyses for Parts A and B of the Trailmaking test, a single analysis was carried out with both parts as a within-subject source of variation. Similar results were found with the additional ones of statistically significant interactions between age and Parts A and B ($p < .01$), and education and Parts A and B ($p < .001$). Increased age and decreased education was associated with a relatively small difference in performance scores between Parts A and B.

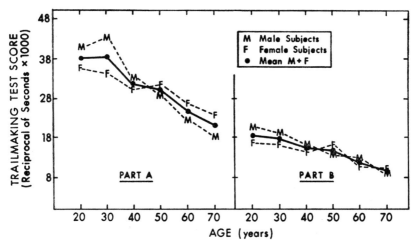

Figure 3.   Mean Trailmaking score as a function of age.

Embedded Figures

Performances related to age and the five difficulty levels of the embedded figures task were compared by an analysis of variance of mixed design. It will be recalled that only women were tested with this procedure, thus not permitting an analysis of sex differences.

It may be seen in Table V that the six age groups differed significantly in their performances ($p < .01$). The general pattern was an age-associated decrease in the percent of problems that were correctly done. It was mostly the two oldest groups, in their relatively poor performances, which contributed much to the significant age effect (see Figure 4). Table V also shows that the five parts of the test differed in difficulty ($p < .0001$); the last two tests were especially difficult, as judged by the mean performance scores. The age groups were similar with respect to the effect of task difficulty, i.e. the interaction between age and difficulty was not statistically significant ($p > .05$).

Higher than twelve years of schooling was associated with better test scores than having had less schooling ($p < .05$) and this was particularly so with the more difficult problems (the

TABLE V

ANALYSIS OF VARIANCE OF EMBEDDED FIGURES TEST DATA

Source	df	MS	F
Between	59		
Educ. (E)	1	9896	5.37§
Age (A)	5	7182	3.90‡
Residual	53	1842	
Within	240		
Diff. (D)	4	21306	69.84†
E X D	4	1101	3.61‡
A X D	20	407	1.33
Residual	212	305	
Total	299		

† $p < .0001$
‡ $p < .01$
§ $p < .05$

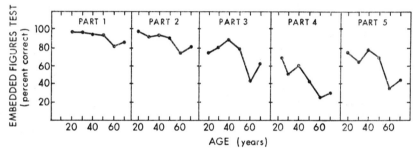

Figure 4.   Mean Embedded Figures Test score as a function of age.

interaction between education level and task difficulty was significant at less than the .01 level).

A multivariate analysis, by age and education, of the five parts of the embedded figures procedure revealed nonsignificant ($p > .05$) multivariate F-ratios associated with the age and the education effects, disallowing interpretation of the individual univariate analyses of each part. However, when Part 5 was ordered first in the multivariate analysis, as the most difficult of the five, the associated step-down F-ratios were statistically significant ($p < .01$) with respect to age and to education. The step-down F-ratios associated with these effects for each of the other parts were not significant ($p > .05$). Thus, Part 5 was seen to account for a significant portion of the variance in terms of performance on the embedded figures task, with the other parts being redundant. The univariate analysis of this portion of the embedded figures procedure revealed a significant age effect ($p < .01$) with the older groups performing more poorly; ω^2 was .19. The estimated performance means for the six age groups of women subjects on Part 5 may be seen in Table IV.

Correlations Among Test Scores

The test scores of the three procedures given to both men and women (VOT, Parts A and B of Trailmaking) were intercorrelated, as were the scores of the four tests given to women only. (The embedded figures test was represented by Part 5, the part associated with most of the variance.) Of the three correlations based upon men and women subjects, and the six correlations based upon only women subjects, none were sizable, the largest being 0.26. Thus, the tests are seen as largely independent, measuring different aspects of brain function.

CONCLUSION

The data of this chapter demonstrated that increasing age was associated with relatively poor performances on tests that have been here called "brain function." They also demonstrated that, depending on the specific task and the sex of subjects, between 10 and 28 percent of performance variance could be accounted for by age. About a fifth of the VOT and Embedded Figures variances could be explained by age, and a tenth of the Trailmaking score could. However, the magnitude of performance decrements with age was appreciable mostly in the later decades. Whatever these tests are called, brain function or otherwise, it was pointed out that they measure behavior involving perceptual ability, not brain physiology.

If we accept as fact that age is one of several determinants of performance on these tests, the VOT indicates that spatial relations are less good with the old than with the young. The

Trailmaking test results suggest that serial planning that involves memory and search declines with age; and the Embedded Figures tasks measuring the ability to perceive forms that are enmeshed in complex contexts similarly show decline. This type of decline may be related to the ability to spot or find what is looked for in the immediate environment or, possibly, in culling information that is embedded in a broader context.

CHAPTER FOUR

PSYCHOMOTOR SPEED

Under the rubric "psychomotor speed," many different kinds of tests may be found. They have in common the requirement that something be done quickly, most often continuously, although not necessarily. Usually, tests of psychomotor speed are simple and require little to master them. When they are complex, they tend to be called something other than tests of psychomotor speed. For example, the Trailmaking tests, both parts A and B described in Chapter 3, contain elements of psychomotor speed. A distinguishing characteristic, perhaps, is in the time spent in performance relative to the time spent in mentation or perception. The more time spent in the former, the more it would tend to be called psychomotor speed.

Three procedures were used in this section. Two were traditional in that they measured how quickly people can carry out simple operations, and one was different in that it measured how slowly this can be done. The two speed tests are very simple, taking only minutes or even seconds to administer. Scores on these tests have been found correlated with age and at least one of them (Copying Digits) was able to differentiate normal from psychotic elderly (Birren and Botwinick, 1951). As indicated in Chapter 1, the decrease with age in the ability to respond quickly is thought by several investigators to be a reflection of central nervous system functioning.

Paradoxically, perhaps, elderly people have not only been found slower in carrying out tasks than young adults, but they have also been found not as slow when required to inhibit normal speed patterns. For example, it was seen in one study that elderly subjects did not write as quickly as did young adult subjects when they were instructed to write quickly, nor did they write as slowly when the instructions called for writing as slowly as possible (Botwinick, Brinley and Robbin, 1959). The elderly were modulated, so to speak, within a relatively narrow band of response speeds.

It has been hypothesized that the elderly benefit from behavioral tempos which are neither very fast nor very slow. The benefit is a minimizing of errors in tasks of continuous performance and of sequential processing of information where the rate of stimulus input is controlled by response speeds. In such continuous and sequential functions, behavior which is not too fast may minimize overload from incoming serial information. Behavior which is not too slow functions to decrease the time intervals between inputs or between behavioral sequences. This may minimize opportunities for decay and interference processes to disturb memory and related functions.

PROCEDURES

Copying Digits

A page of digits (Arabic numbers 1 through 9) was presented to each subject. There were eight digits in a row with twelve rows to the page, making ninety-six digits in all. Digits within a row were approximately one inch apart, and rows were approximately ¾ inch apart. The digits were typed with elite-size characters and underlined.

The subject's job was simply to copy under the line, the digit presented above it. The instruction was to copy the digits as quickly as possible, going from left to right on each row. The score was the number of digits copied over the time taken to copy them. Thus, the score was in terms of digits per second (multiplied by 100 to eliminate decimals). A maximum of three minutes was allowed for this task.

Crossing-Off

This procedure was designed as a simplified version of the Copying Digits task to reduce as much as possible the cognitive or perceptual requirements of the latter task (Botwinick and Storandt, 1973). Horizontal lines, approximately ¼ inch long, were typed in rows of eight each. There were twelve rows, making ninety-six horizontal lines in all. Again, within a row, each unit, i.e. horizontal line, was separated from the other by approximately one inch, and the separation between rows was approximately ¾ inch. Each subject was instructed to make a vertical or diagonal mark across each horizontal line, "as quickly as possible," working from left to right, one row after another. As in Copying Digits, the score was the number of lines "crossed" per second (multiplied by 100), with a maximum of three minutes allowed for the task if the ninety-six lines were not crossed before then.

Slow Writing

Each subject was instructed as follows:

> I want you to write the words "United States" but I want you to write them as slowly as you can. Don't dot your i or cross your t's. Do not lift your pencil from the paper.

Throughout the subject's performance, he was told, "Slower," "As slow as you can," or similar phrases. The score was the time in seconds to complete the task, with a maximum score of five minutes if the task was not yet completed.

RESULTS

A multivariate analysis of variance based on performance scores of the three psychomotor tests, i.e. Copying Digits, Crossing-Off, and Slow Writing, showed statistically significant effects of education, sex, and age ($p < .0001$), as well as significant interaction among these three variables ($p < .025$). These significant results permitted the univariate analyses which follow.

Speed Performances

The step-down analysis of variance in which the test for age effects was made by adjusting for education and sex differences was carried out for each of the three psychomotor procedures. Scores on the two speed tests, Copying Digits and Crossing-Off, were significantly different among the six age groups. Table VI indicates that the age differences were significant at less than the .0001 level, and Figure 5 and Table VII show that the general pattern is one of decreasing speed with increasing age.

TABLE VI

ANALYSES OF VARIANCES OF PSYCHOMOTOR SPEED TASK DATA

Source	df	Copying Digits	Crossing Off	Slow Writing
			Tests	
Educ. (E)	1	45.60†	30.93†	26.03†
Sex (S)	1	0.25	0.11	28.61†
Age (A)	5	11.45†	11.81†	4.08‡
A X S	5	0.87	0.48	2.89§
A X E	5	3.19‡	0.46	0.38
S X E	1	0.92	0.05	0.01
A X S X E	4	0.95	0.95	3.40§
Within*	97	(920.92)	(1241.19)	(5662.46)

* Error term represented by mean squares. All other sources of variation are represented by F-ratios.
† $p < .0001$
‡ $p < .01$
§ $p < .02$

As determined by an ω^2 analysis, the percent of variance accounted for by age in the speed of carrying out these tasks was 23 for Copying Digits and 27 for Crossing-Off. The corresponding values for women subjects alone were 30 and 33.

In neither test was one of the sexes quicker in their performances than the other ($p > .05$), but those subjects with more than twelve years of formal education were quicker than those

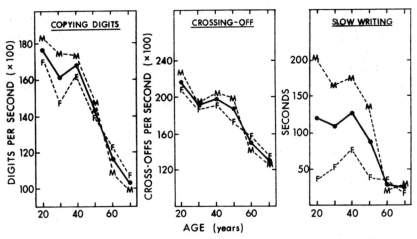

Figure 5. Mean Test Performance score as a function of age. Solid line represents mean of men and women combined. Dashed line represents men (M) or women (F).

with twelve or less years of schooling ($p < .0001$). Only one interaction was statistically significant, that between age and education in the Copying Digits performances ($p < .01$). The combination of youth and high education made for the quickest performances. However, since this interaction was not statistically significant in the multivariate analysis, much emphasis should not be placed on it in the univariate case.

TABLE VII

PSYCHOMOTOR SPEED: ESTIMATED PERFORMANCE
MEANS BY AGE DECADES

Tests	20s	30s	40s	50s	60s	70s
			Age (Years)			
Copying Digits (digits/sec)*	179.7	166.6	161.2	144.8	120.5	108.0
Crossing Off (No./sec)*	216.11	194.9	198.6	188.8	157.8	132.5
Slow Writing	112.0	95.19	118.5	90.8	22.39	20.7
Males	188.5	149.7	163.0	129.7	16.9	23.1
Females	35.5	40.7	74.0	52.0	27.8	18.3

* Multiplied by 100 to eliminate decimals in data recording and analysis.

Slow Writing

Table VI shows statistically significant differences for each of the main effect sources of variation, as well as for the interaction between age and sex. When asked to write as slowly as possible, the elderly subjects seemed to find it particularly hard to comply. While the significant age differences ($p < .01$) were extremely great in magnitude, as may be seen in Figure 5 and Table VII, the ω^2 analysis indicated that only 8 percent of the variance of slow writing performances was accounted for by age.

Males were superior in their performances to females, i.e. the men were very much slower in writing, as per task instructions ($p < .0001; \omega^2 = .14$). These mean sex differences were also great in magnitude; their extent was extraordinary. Men subjects completed the slow writing task in 122.2 seconds (estimated means), as compared to 43.10 seconds for women subjects. A closer analysis, however, showed that this sex difference was mainly or solely with young people—not elderly ones. As seen by the statistically significant interaction in Table VI between age and sex ($p < .02$) and by the data in Table VII and Figure 5, the pattern was one of a steep age decline for males, but not for females. Young women performed about as poorly as did elderly women on this slow writing task.

Again, higher education was associated with better perform-ance, i.e. slow writing, than was lower education ($p < .0001$). The group difference in education was a factor in the interaction between age and sex in slow writing. As seen in Table VI, the second order interaction, that of age, sex, and education, was statistically significant ($p < .02$). In general, middle-aged women of higher education performed well relative to other women subjects, i.e. relative to those of younger and older age and those of lower education of all ages. However, they per-formed less well than men of the same age.

Correlations Among Test Scores

Not surprisingly, performances on the two speed tests were highly correlated, $r = 0.60$ ($p < .01$). Correlations between each of the two speed tests and the slow writing test were not significantly greater than zero.

CONCLUSION

The results of this section corroborate findings of previous studies indicating that, compared to young adults, older people either cannot or do not carry out tasks quickly when the test situation requires it, nor do they carry out tasks with response tempos much slower than is habitual when this is required. It was pointed out that the slowing of responses may have its antecedents in central nervous system age changes, and the narrowing of the range of response speeds within which older people function may have the beneficial effect of minimizing errors in performance.

There was an unexpected result in the present study which may challenge the latter part of this thinking, at least as it implies an involuntary system. The unexpected result was the sex difference in slow writing speed: the men were able to stretch out their normal writing speeds so that they took about three times as long as did the women to write the words, United States (122 vs. 43 seconds). In addition, age differences were much greater for men than for women. For men, there was a systematic decline in slow writing, ranging from approximately 202 seconds (observed means) for subjects aged in their twenties to approximately twenty-eight seconds for those aged in their seventies. The age pattern for women was unsystematic, ranging from seventy-seven seconds for those aged in their forties to seventeen seconds for the subjects in their seventies. Women in their twenties took only thirty-nine seconds for this task.

In view of these results, additional or alternate hypotheses may be in order. Reviewing the slow writing data, it would seem that the unique groups in terms of performance were the young men. They followed instructions and carried out the task as required. All other subjects, i.e. young women and older people of both sexes, tended to not do this, certainly not nearly as well.

Subjectively, the task is uncomfortable, in that to do it well it is necessary to control natural or habitual tendencies. There is frustration and boredom in moving the pencil ever so slowly; seconds seem long and minutes can feel unending. It may be that for some subjects, young women and aged people particularly, the necessary self-control may just not be worth the price for successful task accomplishment. For these subjects, their scores may be a reflection of what Hulicka (1967, p. 180) reported for many of her aged subjects in a paired-associate learning experiment: "Many refused . . . to exert themselves . . . (for) 'such nonsense.' . . ." Perhaps the slow writing task is more a measure of compliance with experimenter demands than it is a test of ability of motor control.

CHAPTER FIVE

INTELLIGENCE

It was indicated in Chapter 1 that cross-sectional studies of intelligence, and perhaps longitudinal studies as well, disclose a classic aging pattern. Verbal functions, especially when related to past achievements, hold up well in later life; but perceptual-integrative functions, the processing of new information, especially when involving speed of response, do not hold up well. These latter functions decline with age, particularly with people of low intellectual ability in young adulthood.

This aging pattern was disclosed largely by research with the most frequently used test of adult intelligence—the Wechsler Adult Intelligence Scale (WAIS). This test is composed of eleven subtests, each measuring different, but related, aspects of intelligence (Wechsler, 1955). The present study uses four of the eleven subtests: Vocabulary, Comprehension, Block Design, and Picture Arrangement. The former two subtests are among those which measure functions holding with age, and the latter two, i.e. Block Design and Picture Arrangement, measure functions which do not. An analysis of ten studies based on a variety of different types of subjects showed a remarkable consistency in the ordering of functions holding with age. Among the eleven subtests, Vocabulary and Comprehension ranked two and three, respectively, and Block Design and Picture Arrangement, nine and ten, respectively (Botwinick, 1967, p. 9).

The above refers to what sometimes is called normal aging. The pattern for a combination of normal aging and psychoses of the senium is different. With senile deterioration, the Comprehension and Picture Arrangement functions decline over and beyond normal aging, while Vocabulary and Block Design do so to a much lesser degree (Botwinick, 1973).

PROCEDURES

Five procedures were used in the assessment of intelligence. In addition to the four WAIS subtests, one other that was given is part of a personality test described in Chapter 6, viz. the 16 PF. This personality test measures sixteen dimensions of personality, one being intelligence. Since this dimension is more appropriate to the present discussion than to personality, it was separated from the other fifteen and covered here. The type of questions and the context making up the 16 PF suggest that this aspect of intelligence may be different from that measured by the more frequently used intelligence tests.

Vocabulary

The WAIS subtests are so well known that only very brief descriptions will be given here. The Vocabulary test comprises a list of forty words, presented one at a time in a general order of difficulty. With each word orally presented, the subject attempts a definition. A good definition is scored 2; a poor one is scored 1; an incorrect one or a failure to attempt a definition is scored zero. After five consecutive zero scores, the test is terminated. The total score is then converted to a scaled score, based upon a statistical normalizing procedure. In fact, all WAIS subtest scores are converted to scaled scores.

Comprehension

The comprehension test is made up of fourteen questions, each related to common experience. The questions bear on a wide variety of topics, asking the purpose of an event or activity, and "what" is the thing to do when a certain event occurs. Understanding social factors and their consequences, and personal judgments are measured by this test. As with the Vocabulary test, each item is scored 2, 1, or zero.

Block Design

Block Design is a test which involves making the same patterns or designs with blocks as are depicted on two-dimensional card drawings. Each block is approximately one inch in every dimension. Each side of the block is painted in either one color (red or white), or in two colors (red and white) with each color forming an isosceles triangle. The designs that are formed are not by building the blocks one upon the other but by placing colors one along side the other.

There are ten designs to be made, each with time limits imposed for completing them. The first two designs are simple; they earn scores of either 4, 2, or zero depending upon whether they are done correctly in a first or second try. The next four designs earn 4 or zero points depending upon whether they are done correctly within the time limit. The last four earn 4 or zero points, plus one or two additional points as time bonuses if they are done correctly quickly. The total score is an addition of all the points.

Picture Arrangement

The Picture Arrangement test comprises eight series of several cards each. The cards are of comic strip type characters, drawn in black on white cards. If the cards in each series are arranged in a correct order or sequence, they tell a story or describe a situation, much as does the newspaper comic strip that doesn't have captions or dialogue. If the arrangement is not in a correct order, there is no meaningful story or situation.

The cards in each series are presented to the subject in mixed order and the subject attempts to order them meaningfully. Time limits are imposed on each of the eight series with bonuses for correct orders done quickly. The scoring is similar in some ways to that of Block Design.

PF

Chapter 6 gives details about this test. Here, it will only be indicated that a series of written statements are presented to each subject, who responds by choosing one among three alternatives that refer to the statement. Most often the alternatives take some form of true, false, or in-between. With respect to Factor B (Intelligence), however, the items take the form of analogies such as, woman is to child as cat is to: a. kitten, b. dog, c. boy.

RESULTS

The vocabulary subtest was given to both men and women subjects, the other four were given to women only. A multivariate analysis of variance based upon the performance scores of women taking all five procedures showed statistically significant effects of age ($p < .0001$) and education ($p < .01$), but not of the interaction between these two sources of variation ($p > .05$). These results permitted univariate analyses of the test scores which are described below.

Vocabulary

The Vocabulary univariate analysis highlighted the conservatism of the step-down least-squares solution with respect to age effects. It may be seen in Table VIII that the step-down

TABLE VIII

ANALYSES OF VARIANCE OF VOCABULARY TEST RESPONSES

Source	df	MS	F
Educ. (E)	1	119.7	23.10†
Sex (S)	1	36.7	7.08‡
Age (A)	5	11.1	2.14
A X S	5	5.6	1.08
Residual	107	5.2	
Total	119		

Note: Age differences were not statistically significant in this analysis ($p > .05$). However, when age was ordered first in the step-down analysis, age differences were significant ($p < .01$).
† $p < .0001$
‡ $p < .01$

analysis in which education and sex were ordered first and second, respectively, age differences were not significant ($p > .05$). However, in the analysis where age was ordered first, before sex and education, age differences were significant ($p < .01$). In the former case, the contribution of age was adjusted for the effects of education and sex; in the latter case, age was left unadjusted, i.e. the intrinsic confound between age and education was left in the data. The percent of test score variance

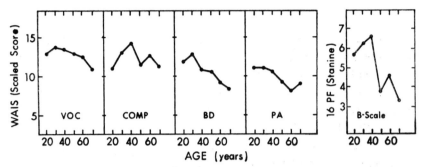

Figure 6.   Mean performance scores as a function of age.

(ω^2) accounted for by age when ordered first was 9; that by education, 14.

Not surprisingly, those subjects with more than twelve years of formal schooling performed better in the Vocabulary test than those who had twelve or less years ($p < .0001$). Women performed better than men ($p < .01$), but there was no significant interaction between age and sex ($p > .05$). Figure 6 shows the observed means by age decades, while Table IX shows the estimated Vocabulary scores.

TABLE IX

INTELLIGENCE: ESTIMATED PERFORMANCE
MEANS BY AGE DECADES

	Age (Years)					
Tests	*20s*	*30s*	*40s*	*50s*	*60s*	*70s*
WAIS (scaled score)						
Voc	12.35	13.05	13.05	12.99	13.09	11.17
Comp	10.97	12.59	14.17	11.78	12.65	11.17
BD	11.64	11.95	10.74	10.99	9.43	8.14
PA	11.10	11.01	10.50	9.30	8.00	9.00
16 PF (Stanine)						
B	5.60	5.92	6.50	4.09	4.79	3.20

Comprehension

Table X shows statistically significant age effects with the Comprehension scale. The significance level, however, was not great ($p < .04$) and the age pattern was not monotonic; peak perlormance was in the middle years with poorer performances during the earlier and later years (see Table IX). The ω^2 analysis showed that in this unsystematic relationship, age of the subject accounted for 11 percent of the test score variance. Again, education groups were significantly different ($p < .03$), with high test scores associated with the higher education level.

The estimated means may be seen in Table IX and the observed means in Figure 6.

TABLE X

ANALYSES OF VARIANCES OF THREE WAIS SUBTEST
SCORES AND FACTOR B OF THE 16 PF

			Tests		
Source	df	Comp	BD	PA	PF-B
Educ.	1	5.31§	16.32‡	1.52	13.79‡
Age	5	2.64**	5.55‡	2.68**	6.50†
Residual*	53	(5.28)	(3.68)	(5.20)	(2.22)
Total	59				

* Residuals are represented by mean squares. All other sources of variations are represented by F-ratios.
† $p < .0001$
‡ $p < .001$
§ $p < .03$
** $p < .04$

Block Design

The analysis of variance of the Block Design data (Table X) disclosed both significant age ($p < .0001$) and education ($p < .001$) effects. The ω^2 analysis showed that 23 percent of the performance variance was explained by age. However, Table IX and Figure 6 show that it is mainly with the two oldest age groups where performance decrement was seen.

Picture Arrangement

The results of the variance analysis of the Picture Arrangement data (Table X) are interesting in that, while age differences were statistically significant ($p < .04$), education differences were not ($p > .05$). The relative independence of test scores and education effects was not to be expected on the basis of previous reports. This will be discussed later.

The age pattern, as seen by the means shown in Table IX and Figure 6, was general decline. As determined by ω^2, 12 percent of the performance variance was accounted for by age.

PF

Scale B of the sixteen Personality Factor test—the intelligence scale—when subjected to the step-down variance analysis (see Table X) disclosed significant age ($p < .0001$) and education ($p < .001$) effects. Table IX shows the estimated means as related to age, and Figure 6 shows the observed means. In general, as age increased, performance on this test decreased. Twenty-seven percent of the variance could be explained by age (ω^2). Higher education was associated with higher test scores.

Correlations Among Test Scores

The five test scores were intercorrelated and four correlations were found statistically significant at less than the .01 level, and two at less than the .05 level. The highest correlations were among Vocabulary, Comprehension, and Block Design. They ranged from 0.41 to 0.47. The other correlation significant at less than the .01 level was between Picture Arrangement and Block Design; $r = 0.35$.

CONCLUSION

The Vocabulary and Comprehension subtests of the WAIS were selected for use in this study because functions measured by these scales are known to be maintained with advancing adult age. The Block Design and Picture Arrangement subtests were selected for just the opposite reason, i.e. they measure functions which decrease with age—at least as measured cross-sectionally. The results of the present study were mainly, but not totally, in agreement with these generalizations.

The Vocabulary data were seen as largely a function of education level. This is in accord with several reports, most notably, perhaps, that of Birren and Morrison (1961). The Comprehension data, while statistically significant with respect to age, were so at only the .04 level. With as many statistical tests as made in the present investigation, perhaps a more stringent criterion of statistical significance ought to be adopted. Table IX shows that whatever the reliability of the age effect in Comprehension performance, the magnitude of the effect was not great.

The Block Design results followed expectations, i.e. advanced age was associated with relatively poor performance. The Picture Arrangement data, however, were not completely in line with what the literature suggests. Ranking tenth of eleven subtests in age patterning (see Table 1, p. 9 of Botwinick, 1967), the expectation would be that age differences in Picture Arrangement would be both very highly statistically significant and large in magnitude. This was not the case.

It was indicated that the education effect was not found with the Picture Arrangement data. This is contrary to what might be expected since education level was seen important with respect to responses on all subtests of the WAIS. Birren and Morrison reported correlations between education and Vocabulary, Comprehension, Block Design and Picture Arrangement test scores as follows: 0.62, 0.52, 0.44, and 0.49, respectively. Their report indicated that education level accounted for more of the variance associated with intelligence than did age.

The results with the intelligence scale of the 16 PF (Scale B) were in support of results already reported in the literature (e.g. Fozard and Nuttall, 1971). Increased age was associated with decreased performance. In the present study, age appeared to contribute more to the performance variance than educational level, as determined by the relative sizes of the respective mean squares when age and education were each ordered first in the step-down analyses. Conceptually, this may be in partial variance with the report of Fozard and Nuttall that education weighed more heavily than age in test performance (discriminant function coefficients were greater for socioeconomic status than for age). Since Factor B of the 16 PF is thought to measure crystallized (learned) intelligence, as opposed to fluid (genetic) intelligence (e.g. Cattell et al., 1970; Ross, 1970), Fozard and Nuttall's emphasis on nonmaturational antecedents of test performances may be the correct one.

Taken together, the results of the present study support the literature indicating that elderly subjects perform relatively poorly on some intellectual tasks but not on all of them. Performances on Block Design and PF showed most of the age decline, with age accounting for about one quarter of the performance variance with each task.

CHAPTER SIX

PERSONALITY/MORALE

U NLIKE THE PRESENT investigation, most studies on memory do not include analysis of personality data. Not that it is necessarily to be expected that personality and morale have important bearing on memory, but neither is it to come as a surprise if learned that they do. Should it be seen that they do, it would remain to be determined whether age-related personality differences are the basis of cognitive age differences or whether personality and morale are the consequences of changing cognitive abilities. Perhaps both personality and cognitive age differences derive from common antecedents.

PROCEDURES

Four procedures were used to assess personality and morale. They were: 1) the short form (Form C) of the Cattell 16 Personality Factor Test (commonly called the 16 PF), 2) the Depression Scale (D-Scale) of the Minnesota Multiphasic Personality Inventory (MMPI), 3) a rating scale of life satisfaction, and 4) a rating scale of feeling in control of oneself and one's social world. This battery of tests was meant to assess much of what is important in personality study, especially in regard to aging adults.

16 PF

This test was developed with the aid of factor analysis (Cattell, Eber and Tatsuoka, 1970). Sixteen personality factors were determined; thus the name of the test. The short form of the test used here is composed of 105 statements, each followed by three alternative choices. For example, one statement might be, "Money cannot bring happiness." The alternative choices might be yes (or true), no (or false), or sometimes (or in-between, occasionally). Alternative choices for some statements are specific to the statement, rather than general as above. In each case, however, they are clear. The 105 statements are preceded by four example statements to make sure the instructions are understood. The instructions read by each subject are: "Inside this booklet are some questions to see what attitudes and interests you have. There are no right and wrong answers. . . ."

One factor of the 16 PF, factor B, is an intelligence factor. The results bearing on this factor were reported in Chapter 5. The results bearing on fifteen factors are reported here.

D-Scale, MMPI

Depression is thought to be very prominent in later life, thus, the MMPI D-Scale was administered. The format of the MMPI is similar in some ways to that of the 16 PF. There are statements to be read and the instruction is to choose among alternatives. The MMPI (Hathaway and McKinley, 1956), in its original form, consists of many cards, each with one statement written on it. The task is simply to read each statement and to place it in one of three categories as it applies: True, False, or Cannot Say. From these responses, a variety of personality characteristics are described; one among these is depression.

The depression scale, or D-scale as it is often called, is made up of sixty statements. Only these were used in the present study. The sixty statements were typed, not individually on cards, but together on regular-size typewriting paper. Each of the sixty D-scale statements was followed by the letters T and F, for true and false. The subject read instructions which included the following: "Read each statement and decide whether it is *true as applied to you or false as applied to you.* You are to circle *T* if the statement is TRUE or MOSTLY TRUE as applied to you. You are to circle *F* if the statement is FALSE or MOSTLY FALSE as applied to you."

As an example, one statement among the sixty is: "I wish I could be as happy as others seem to be." At face value, most of the statements do not appear to be nearly as related to depression as this one.

Life Satisfaction Scale

This scale is a variant of one described as "a pictorial, non-verbal . . . ten-point ladder" (Kilpatrick and Cantril, 1960, p. 159). The ladder is simply a drawing of two vertical lines (about 6.5 inches), with twelve evenly spaced horizontal ones in between. The two vertical lines are 2⅛ inches apart, describing the dimensions of the horizontal lines (i.e. the rungs). The space between the two bottom rungs is labeled 0; the space between the two top rungs is labeled 10, with the spaces in between labeled accordingly. Each separation, then, is a scale choice, with eleven scale alternatives.

Any statement or series of statements may be applied to this scale. In the present investigation the following was written beneath the drawing of the ladder:

> Some people seem to be quite happy and satisfied with their lives, while others seem quite unhappy and dissatisfied. Now look at the ladder. Suppose that a person who is entirely satisfied with his life would be at the top of the ladder, and a person who is extremely dissatisfied with his life would be at the bottom of the ladder. Where would you put yourself on the ladder at the present stage of your life in terms of how satisfied or dissatisfied you are with your own personal life? Circle the number.

Control Rating Scale

The ladder, just described, is not the traditional way of obtaining self-rating data. A more traditional way is either a verbal instruction similar to that with the 16 PF or the MMPI or the use of a horizontal line rather than vertical ones.

In the present study, the control rating scale was in the form of a horizontal line, 5½ inches long. Diagonal slash marks equally spaced across the line were numbered 0 through 10. Beginning underneath the zero, the word None was typed; centered underneath the 5, the word "Medium"; and beginning under the 9 and extending beyond the 10, the word "Excellent" was typed.

The instructions to the subject were presented immediately above this scale. They read:

Most people have a general idea about what being in control of things means. On the scale below, 10 indicates excellent control, 5 indicates medium control, and 0 indicates no control. Circle a number showing how you rate yourself on control. What degree of control do you feel you have over things? Circle a number and tell me.

RESULTS

The rating scale of life satisfaction and the rating scale of feeling in control were given to both men and women, while the PF and D-scale were given to women subjects only. Multivariate analyses of variances were carried out both with the performance scores of women subjects taking all four tests (each of the fifteen scores of the PF plus the three others), and with the fifteen PF scores alone. In neither case was statistical significance achieved in regard to either the effect of age or of education ($p > .05$). A multivariate analysis of the two rating scale data similarly showed a lack of statistical significance of the effects of age, education, and sex ($p > .05$). Strictly speaking, therefore, further analyses of the individual measures are not indicated. Univariate analyses were carried out despite this, largely to see how some of the present data compared with those of previous reports.

15 PF

None of the fifteen univariate analyses of variances of the PF scores indicated age effects significant at the .01 level. Only factor N (forthright-shrewd) resulted in age differences significant at less than the .05 level when age was ordered last in the step-down analyses (see Table XI). With as many statistical tests as made in this study, conclusions based upon confidence levels of 5 percent must remain equivocal at best. When age was ordered first in the step-down analyses, three other factors were seen as significant at less than the .05 level: Factors E (submissiveness), G (Superego strength) and H (shy-venturesome).

An examination of the age group estimated means shows the basic normality of the subjects in all age groups (see Table XII).

TABLE XI

ANALYSES OF VARIANCES OF SCORES ON FACTOR N
OF THE 16 PF AND ON THE MMPI D-SCALE

		Tests	
Source	*df*	*16 PF-N*	*D-Scale*
Educ.	1	0.91	0.01
Age	5	2.41†	0.83
Residual*	53	(4.38)	(30.43)
Total	59		

Note: When age was ordered first in the step-down analysis, Factors E, G, and H of the 16 PF were statistically significant at less than the .05 level with respect to age.
* Residuals are represented by mean squares. All other sources of variation are represented by F-ratios.
† $p < .05$

TABLE XII

PERSONALITY/MORALE: ESTIMATED PERFORMANCE
MEANS BY AGE DECADES

	Age (Years)					
Tests	*20s*	*30s*	*40s*	*50s*	*60s*	*70s*
16 PF (Stanine)						
E	5.23	6.63	5.43	5.10	5.73	4.53
G	5.59	4.65	5.69	5.94	6.22	7.49
H	5.84	7.15	6.44	4.59	5.02	4.64
N	5.29	4.25	5.39	6.74	6.33	7.19
D-Scale MMPI	18.88	18.13	20.98	22.45	22.23	20.38
(No. dep. items)						
Life Satis.*	6.85	7.35	8.00	7.76	8.32	7.88
Control Rating*	7.60	7.36	7.60	7.02	7.12	7.46

* Self-rating Scale: 10 is highest satisfaction (control) rating, zero is lowest.

Mean scores of 5 and 6 are considered average with scores lower and higher than this as less average. No mean was as low as 4 and only three reached or exceeded 7. (This held for the observed means as well as the estimated ones.) Table XII shows that subjects in their seventies made high scores on factor scales G and N—they tended toward conscientiousness and shrewdness. Subjects in their thirties scored high on scale H—they tended toward venturesome, spontaneous patterns.

None of the education differences tested for each of the fifteen PF were significant at the .01 level.

D-Scale and Rating Scales

Age differences in performance were not significant ($p > .05$) in regard to the MMPI D-scale (Table XI) nor in regard to each of the two self-rating scales (Table XIII). This was so whether or not age was ordered first in the step-down analysis. Neither were education differences nor sex differences statistically significant ($p > .05$). The estimated performances means in relation to age may be seen in Table XII.

TABLE XIII

ANALYSES OF VARIANCES OF LIFE SATISFACTION RATINGS
AND OF FEELINGS OF BEING IN CONTROL

		Tests	
Source	df	Life Sat.	Control
Educ. (E)	1	0.01	3.64
Sex (S)	1	0.01	0.70
Age (A)	5	1.11	0.33
A X S	5	0.52	0.55
Residual°	107	(4.63)	(3.03)
Total	119		

° Residuals are represented by mean squares. All other sources of variation are represented by F-ratios, none of which are significant at the .05 level.

Correlations Among Test Scores

Five correlations among the test scores of the women subjects were statistically significant ($p = .01$ or less). Of these, four involved the D-scale of the MMPI: As Depression increased, Life Satisfaction tended to decrease ($r = -0.33$), as did feelings of being in Control ($r = -0.40$). Along with increased Depression there was a tendency for increased shyness (Factor H, $r = -0.36$) and decreased naturalness or forthrightness (Factor N, $r = 0.48$). Feelings of being in Control and naturalness (Factor N) also tended to go together ($r = -0.32$). Scores of feelings of being in Control and of Life Satisfaction were significantly correlated in samples of men and women subjects combined ($r = 0.32$), but not women alone ($r = 0.24$).

CONCLUSION

The results of this section may concisely be summarized as follows: Personality as measured here was seen similar from age group to age group. This conclusion is not unlike that of Neugarten, Crotty and Tobin (1964, p. 187) quoted in Chapter 1: "Personality type was independent of age." It is also compatible with one conclusion of a study in which PF age differences were found: "In contrast with the ability tests, the dependence upon variations in scores on the personality measures was much less . . ." (Fozard, 1972, p. 180).

The results of this section are not compatible, however, with all that has been reported in the literature. For example, Fozard and Nuttall (1971) found significant age effects with multivariate analysis of the 16 PF scale data, as well as with several of the factor scale scores. Goodwin and Schaie (1969) also reported significant age differences, although these two studies were not in total agreement as to which of the scales differentiated age groups.[1] The greatest difference between the two studies was with Factor F. Fozard and Nuttall reported that their greatest age effect, and to an appreciable extent, was with this factor: an age decline in surgency, i.e. in a heedless, happy-go-lucky behavior pattern; with age there was greater caution and sobriety. Goodwin and Schaie (1969) did not find an age difference in surgency, but Cattell et al. (1970, p. 87) did.

There are various forms of the 16 PF test and not all studies used the same form. Perhaps this could account for the various results. Perhaps it was the specific age groupings, the fact that only women were tested here, the nature of subject sampling, or of data analysis, that could explain the different findings. In any

---

[1]Fozard and Nuttall reported significant age differences in nine scales: B, E, F, G, I, N, O, Q_2, and Q_3. Goodwin and Schaie reported significant age differences in eight: A, E, H, L, O, Q_2, Q_3, and Q_4. (B, N, and Q were not administered.) Thus, there were only four of the thirteen scales common to both studies in which significant age differences were reported: E, O, Q_2, and Q_3. In the present study, only scales B, E, G, H, and N could be considered significant with respect to age. Comparing the three studies, only scale E among the thirteen PF was significant in each one. The pattern in each of the three studies was increased submissiveness with older age.

case, generalizations as to age based upon the 16 PF scales seem limited.

The MMPI D-scale results were also at variance with previous reports. For example, subjects aged sixty-seven to eighty-seven years had been seen as more depressed ($p < .01$) than subjects aged eighteen to thirty-five (Botwinick and Thompson, 1967). The present study did not disclose significant age differences in mean scale performances despite the use of the exact same test by one of the same investigators.

Self-ratings of life satisfaction were in only partial accord with published results. Bortner and Hultsch (1970) investigated Life Satisfaction with a scale very similar to the one used here and reported statistically significant age differences. They began their report by referring to a variety of studies and writing:

> Life satisfaction, the ratings of individuals in terms of a general appraisal of their life, is a conceptualization initially and still primarily identified with gerontology. . . . (Various) demographic variables such as age . . . have been demonstrated to show systematic relationships to life satisfaction (p. 41).

Bortner and Hultsch not only used a scale very similar to the one used here, their age groupings were similar; the major difference was that their oldest age group was listed as seventy-plus years, rather than seventy to seventy-nine years. As in the present study, they also found that the magnitude of age differences was very small. The percent of their test variance that was explained by the age of the subject was only 0.006—effectively no age effect at all.

The scale assessing feelings of being in control was used in an attempt to investigate a concept thought related to disengagement. Elderly people draw away from others and from activities, and many gerontologists believe that at least part of this disengagement is due more to society's doings than to their own. If this is so, elderly people might be expected to feel a lack of control of activities and directions in the world around them. The present results did not substantiate this thinking.

CHAPTER SEVEN

HEALTH/HABIT

HEALTH AND HEALTH HABITS were assessed by four procedures. Three of them were ratings or responses by the subjects, and one of them was ratings by the investigator. The latter was called Clinical Impression and was designed to assess general well-being. This procedure could have been categorized as easily with personality/morale, discussed in the previous chapter, as with health/habit, as discussed here.

The Clinical Impression score is similar, at least conceptually, to a qualitative score, Senile Quality, found meaningful in a multidisciplinary investigation where many objective tests were given and many measurements were made (Birren et al., 1963). The Senile Quality score was of a global clinical impression involving "cognitive dysfunction, alterations in behavior, and disturbances in affective expression . . ." (Perlin and Butler, 1963, p. 167). The Clinical Impression rating of the present study, while operationally different than the Senile Quality score, had in common with it the goal of categorizing people on a scale of what is often and loosely called, mental health.

In addition to this scale of mental health, a broader index of general and physical health was used, the Cornell Medical Index Health Questionnaire (Brodman, et al., 1949). This index (from here on called the Cornell) is a self-administered questionnaire that attempts to categorize different aspects of health, e.g. cardiovascular, sensory, etc. Thus, in addition to an overall index of health, more specific categories of health are assessed.

As an addendum, possibly another aspect of health, a self-rating scale was given to assess one's own feelings of being or of not being healthy. The Cornell was meant to substitute a doctor's assessment, the self-rating was meant to reflect the subject's self-evaluation.

The fourth scale administered had to do with habits of drinking alcohol and smoking. Part of good health is having good health habits; in fact, long life may be based upon such habits. For example, there is much scientific evidence that smoking bears on health and longevity (e.g. U.S. PHS report, 1964). Several studies have pointed to smoking as one of the few items of information, among many, which separated survivor from nonsurvivor groups (e.g. Bartko, Patterson and Butler, 1971). It is reasonable that alcohol consumption may also be important in this way to health and longevity. With this in mind, a questionnaire of such habits was given to each subject.

PROCEDURES

As already indicated, the subjects were rated for Clinical Impression, given two health questionnaires, and asked about drinking and smoking habits. This battery of procedures was designed to evaluate health status and health habits.

Clinical Impression

To make the assessment of clinical impression as objective as possible, and to provide common criteria for the several data collectors of this study, each of twenty-two specific questions was answered yes or no by the person who tested the subject. The twenty-two questions may be seen in Appendix B; they refer to affect states, neurotic behavior, and other aspects of mental health.

The score of Clinical Impression was the number of positive impressions; the higher the score the better the mental health the subject was thought to have.

Cornell

This questionnaire may well be the most widely used of all pencil-and-paper health questionnaires; it has been reported as yielding "correct comprehensive general medical . . . diagnostic evaluation of patients" (Brodman et al., 1953, p. 339). There is a different Cornell form for men and for women. The form for women comprises 195 statements to each of which the subject draws a circle around the word Yes or around the word No, as it applies to her. As indicated, the responses are scored in terms of diagnostic categories. There are eighteen such categories, as, for example, sensory ("Do you need glasses to read?") or cardiovascular ("Does your heart often race like mad?").

Health Rating

The self-rating of general or overall health was ascertained by a horizontal line, divided into ten equal units. This line was presented to each subject with the following instructions: "10 indicates excellent health, 5 indicates average health, 0 indicates poor health. Circle a number showing how you rate yourself in health. What do you think your present health is? Circle a number to tell me."

The scale is identical to the Control Rating Scale described in detail in the previous chapter. Both scales were presented to the subject on the same sheet of paper. The only difference between the scales was that the words, Poor and Average, were markers for the Health Rating Scale, whereas the words, None and Medium, were markers for the Control Rating Scale.

Health Questionnaire

Two health habits were questioned—one of smoking and one of drinking alcohol. Responses were scored from 1 to 4, based upon the extent of habit. No smoking (drinking) and never having done this regularly was scored 4. Past habits but no longer smoking (drinking) was scored 3. Ten or more cigarettes per day (more than 35 oz. liquor per week) was scored 1, with regular consumption less than this amount scored 2. (See Appendix B for items of the questionnaire.)

RESULTS

The Cornell and the health questionnaire were given to women subjects only; the other two procedures were given to both men and women. The Cornell, in its eighteen subparts, was subjected to a multivariate analysis of variance. The other procedures were analyzed individually.

Clinical Impression

It may be seen in Table XIV that education and sex differences were statistically significant ($p < .001$) but not age differ-

TABLE XIV

ANALYSES OF VARIANCES OF EXPERIMENTER'S IMPRESSIONS
OF HEALTH AND OF SUBJECTS' SELF-RATINGS

Source	df	Tests Clin. Imp.	Health Rating
Educ. (E)	1	13.36†	9.97‡
Sex (S)	1	14.48†	0.19
Age (A)	5	0.34	1.06
A X S	5	3.49‡	0.37
Residual*	107	(3.93)	(3.33)
Total	119		

* Residuals are represented by mean squares. All other sources of variations are represented by F-ratios.
† $p < .001$
‡ $p < .01$

ences ($p > .05$). Significant age differences were not found even when age effects were ordered first in the step-down analysis.

Table XIV shows that there was a significant interaction between age and sex ($p < .01$). The nature of this interaction may be seen in Figure 7: Elderly men subjects appeared to the testers as being somewhat less adequate in mental health than younger men, while with women the clinical impressions were less clear. Women subjects in their fifties and sixties appeared less adequate than younger women, but those in their seventies, if anything, appeared more adequate. Overall, however, the differences among age-sex groupings were small. The estimated means by age group are shown in Table XV.

Cornell

A multivariate analysis was carried out with the scores relating to the eighteen diagnostic categories. With education ordered first and age ordered second in the step-down analysis, education group differences were not statistically significant ($p > .05$),

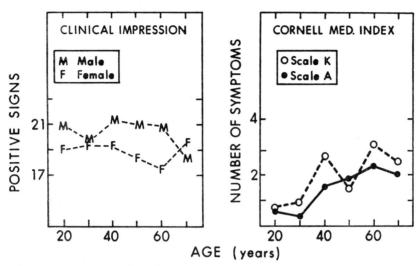

Figure 7. Mean Clinical Impression ratings and Cornell scores as a function of age.

TABLE XV

HEALTH/HABIT: ESTIMATED PERFORMANCE
MEANS BY AGE DECADES

			Age (Years)			
Tests	20s	30s	40s	50s	60s	70s
Clin. Imp. (No. pos. signs)	19.87	19.83	20.27	19.79	19.41	19.36
Cornell A (No. complaints)	0.53	0.44	1.63	1.80	2.23	2.03
Cornell K (No. complaints)	0.63	1.03	2.83	1.40	3.04	2.53
Health Rating (*)	8.27	8.13	7.92	7.79	6.97	7.81
Smoking (**)	3.00	2.19	3.00	3.00	3.40	3.80
Drinking (**)	2.22	2.30	2.12	2.02	2.15	3.12

* Self rating: 10 is best health and zero is poorest.
** Rating of extent of habit: a score of 4 represents no smoking (drinking alcohol) and a score of 1 represents much smoking (drinking).

nor were the age effects significant ($p < .06$); with age ordered first, the significance level for age was less than .03. Univariate analyses were then carried out for each of the eighteen diagnostic categories and for the total of these to determine age effects confounded with those of education level. Of these nineteen analyses, only two showed statistically significant age differences, both at less than the .01 level. The analyses associated with these two procedures, section A (seeing and hearing) and section K (miscellaneous diseases), may be seen in Table XVI.

Figure 7 shows that self reports regarding sensory defects increased with age. This was certainly so beginning at age forty for those with twelve or less years of formal schooling. For those with more than twelve years, the pattern, while less regular, points in the same direction. Young women of the higher education level and those of higher education generally reported more sensory defects. The age pattern on scale K was similar to that of scale A—beginning at age forty, medical difficulties increased. With both these scales, ω^2 analyses indicated that 20 percent of the variance of the questionnaire responses were associated with the age effect.

Health Rating

Table XIV discloses that subjects within the different age groups did not rate themselves very differently in terms of general

TABLE XVI

ANALYSES OF VARIANCES OF RESPONSES TO
HEALTH QUESTIONNAIRES

		Tests			
Source	*df*	*A*	*K*	*Smok.*	*Drink.*
Educ.	1	7.73†	2.12	0.68	0.53
Age	5	4.37†	4.14†	2.77‡	2.74‡
Residual*	53	(1.22)	(2.44)	(0.97)	(0.58)
Total	59				

Note: Tests A and K are the only sections of the 18 constituting the Cornell Medical Index Health Questionnaire on which age groups differed significantly.
* Residuals are represented by mean squares. All other sources of variation are represented by F-ratios.
† $p < .01$
‡ $p < .03$

health ($p > .05$). When, however, age was ordered first in the step-down analysis, age groups were significantly different, but only at less than the .05 level. As indicated in several places throughout this book, this level is probably insufficiently stringent as a criterion of significance in view of the many statistical tests that were made.

Table XV shows that what age differences there may be in self-rating of health, they are in the expected direction, with possible exception of the oldest group. That is, ratings decrease with age up to seventy years and then, possibly, there is a reversal in pattern. Perhaps the standard or expectation changes in the seventies and what people might regard as poor health earlier in life is accepted as all right or good.

Those with more than twelve years of schooling rated themselves as being in better health than those with twelve or less years of schooling ($p < .01$). Men and women were similar in their self-ratings of health ($p > .05$).

Habits Questionnaire

Only women subjects were examined for their drinking and smoking habits. Table XVI shows significant age differences in regard to both these habits ($p < .03$). Education group differences were not significant ($p > .05$).

The estimated mean habit scores are shown in Table XV. It is seen that, in general, younger women disclosed more smoking and more drinking behavior than did older women. The ω^2 analyses indicated that 13 percent of the variance of each of these behaviors was age-related.

Correlations Among Test Scores

The scores for women on smoking and drinking, Health Rating, Clinical Impression, and Scales A and K of the Cornell were intercorrelated. Only one coefficient of correlation was significant at the .01 level—that between Cornell K (miscellaneous diseases) and Health Rating ($r = -0.33$). Not surprisingly, good health assessments tend to go with a history of few illnesses.

CONCLUSION

In one form or another, the four procedures used in this section are rating scales. The Clinical Impression is a rating by the tester, the three others are self-ratings by the person tested. Of these, the Cornell is the only standardized procedure for which there are norms. Thus, conclusions based upon the results of this section must consider the possible unreliability of the rating scales, particularly the untried ones.

The data seem more impressive in regard to the similarity of responses among the age groups than to the difference. The testers did not see older adults as different in mental health than younger adults, and subjects of all ages tended to see themselves of rather good health. On the Cornell, age differences, when present, were confined to seeing and hearing ability and to having had miscellaneous diseases. The latter could well be a simple matter of the older people, having lived more years, had greater opportunity to develop a history of illness (rather than being sicker at the present time).

These results are in contrast to those of Brodman et al. (1953) who reported that older subjects had more overall bodily complaints than younger ones. The differences between the Brodman et al. (1953) results and the present ones might be accounted for by the more sophisticated statistical methods available now and used here. Perhaps more important is the matter of subject selection. The subjects of Brodman et al. were outpatients in a hospital, while those in the present study were selected outside of medical facilities. Moreover, the present subjects were selected for socioeconomic homogeneity and for testability. They had to be able to take a long battery of tests. Perhaps the similarity in health states among the age groups reflects these subject selection criteria.

It was already indicated that self-ratings of health by people of different ages may be based upon different standards and expectations. The same may be true of the tester ratings, even though effort was made to minimize this by quantifying the Clinical Impression scale. The apparent similarity in tester and health self-ratings among the different age groups may not reflect actual health differences. What a seventy-year-old calls good health or a medical symptom, and what a tester regards as good mental health of this seventy-year-old, may be quite different from that of a twenty-year-old.

An argument can be made that the age groups were different in regard to their self-ratings of health, but that this difference was rooted more in sociocultural considerations than in maturational ones. Age differences were significant at less than the 5 percent level when age was ordered first in the step-down analysis. The general trend was for decreased health ratings with increased age, but not, perhaps, including the very oldest group (those in their seventies). If this latter result is a reliable observation, then either the acceptance of a less stringent criterion of good health is typical at this late stage of life or it may be a reflection of the survival of the very fit. Many of those in their fifties and sixties who are of poor health may not survive long beyond age seventy. Thus, those aged seventy to seventy-nine may, in fact, be in better health than many who are aged sixty to sixty-nine years or even younger.

CHAPTER EIGHT

AGE-RELATED BEHAVIOR: SUMMARY AND PRINCIPAL COMPONENT ANALYSIS

THE PRECEDING FIVE chapters dealt with studies of various types of behavior in relation to the age, sex, and education level of the subject. In general, both advanced age and low education were associated with relatively poor test performances, while the sex of the subject was not importantly related.

There were many exceptions to this over-generalized summary, which, in themselves, may be as important as the positive results which were found. Here, however, the statistically significant age differences were the focus of interest. As indicated in Chapter 2, the age differences must be interpreted with a special type of caution. When the performances of people of different ages are compared and found different statistically, the explanation accounting for the finding must include emphasis on both age or maturational factors and on cultural factors. This is so because older people were born and raised in different eras than younger people; thus, their opportunities and experiences were different. An observed age difference, therefore, confounds maturational and cultural factors.

Effort was made in the present study to minimize cultural effects so that the observed age differences might be seen as having greater basis in maturational change. Chapter 2 discussed how this was done; it was noted that the cultural effects were not eliminated, only minimized.

SUMMARY (CHAPTERS 3 THROUGH 7)

Table XVII summarizes the results of all the studies reported thus far, providing information of overall age effects only, not of the other important sources of behavioral variation. The main variance analyses (hierarchical design), in minimizing the role of culture (education) in the test for age differences, provided conservative estimates of the age effects. Levels of statistically significant age differences would have been found greater had age and education been treated as independent, unrelated effects, as is typically done.

TABLE XVII

SUMMARY OF AGE DIFFERENCES IN PERFORMANCE
(Chapters 3 through 7)

Procedures	Chapter	Age Differences (p)	ω^2	Subjects
Brain Function/Perception	3			
VOT (Hooper)		<.0001	.22	M & W
Trailmaking A		<.01	.10	M & W
Trailmaking B		<.01	.10	M & W
Embedded Figure (Part 5)		<.01	.19	W
Psychomotor	4			
Copying Digits		<.0001	.23	M & W
Crossing-Off		<.0001	.27	M & W
Slow Writing		<.01	.08	M & W
Intelligence	5			
Vocabulary		<.01*	.09*	M & W
Comprehension		<.04	.11	W
Block Design		<.0001	.23	W
Picture Arrangement		<.04	.12	W
16 PF (B-scale)		<.0001	.27	W
Personality/Morale	6			
16 PF (N-scale)**		<.05	.11	W
(E-scale)		<.05*	.11*	W
(G-scale)		<.05*	.11*	W
(H-scale)		<.05*	.16*	W
D-scale		Not sig.		W
Life Satisfaction		Not sig.		M & W
Control Rating		Not sig.		M & W
Health/Habit	7			
Clinical Impression		Not sig.		M & W
Cornell (A)**		<.01*	.20*	W
Cornell (K)		<.01*	.20*	W
Health Rating		<.05*	.06*	M & W
Smoking		<.03	.13	W
Drinking		<.03	.13	W

* Statistically significant age effect only when age ordered first in the step-down analysis. ω^2 based on age ordered first.

** Scales of the 16 PF and Cornell not listed here failed to reflect significant age differences even when age was ordered first in the step-down analysis. In the principal component analysis (see text), the total Cornell score was used, not those of scales A and K.

Table XVII also gives information of ω^2. It is one thing to say that the effects are statistically significant; it is quite another thing to say that the age of the subject accounts for much of the performance variance. The ω^2 analyses tell about this latter aspect. Table XVII indicates that even when the age effect was statistically significant, the percentage of performance variance accounted for by age was never larger than 27 and, in most instances, smaller than 10—sometimes much smaller. Higher ω^2 estimates were seen in instances when only the data of women subjects were analyzed. For example, the VOT data of Chapter 3 showed an ω^2 of .28, and the Crossing-Off data of Chapter 4 showed an ω^2 of .33. But, in the main, the ω^2 estimates were not especially high.

Focusing on the many small estimates, say those of 10 percent or even less, may seem discouraging until two important facts are realized. The first is that the computation of ω^2 was based upon the hierarchical analyses of variances that were performed. If these analyses were conservative, so were the ω^2s; other, less conservative, variance analyses may well have indicated greater relationships between age and performance. The second is that it is important to recognize that most behaviors are influenced by multiple factors, not just one. If age is found to account for 10 percent of the variance, an appreciable job of discovery has been accomplished. If several other factors can be isolated, each accounting for 10 percent, the correlates of the performances would be well indicated. An accounting of 10 percent may be thought of as an important step in understanding.

The data of Chapters 3 through 7 may be briefly summarized in this way: Personality and health factors were not very different among the six age groups, if they were different at all. On the other hand, measures of brain function/perception, intelligence, and psychomotor speed reflected age differences; they did so by accounting for approximately 10 to 25 percent of performance variation. This realm of function, therefore, appears to be important to investigate in the study of adult aging.

PRINCIPAL COMPONENT ANALYSES

Cattell (1952) provided a rule of thumb as to the ratio of the minimum number of subjects needed for the measurements that are made in order to carry out a principal component analysis. He indicated that for each measurement there needs to be at least four subjects. This rule was followed here, but only after exploratory analyses were done first.

Table XVII lists twenty-five procedures that were given to the subjects in this study. Not listed in this table are four parts of the Embedded Figures Task and those parts of the Cornell and 16 PF which did not reflect significant age effects in any analysis. While all these procedures were given to women subjects, it may be seen in the table that only eleven were given to both men and women. This made for a problem in data analysis jects was well within the Cattell guideline.

There were 120 men and women subjects; thus, there was no difficulty in regard to the eleven measurements. The eleven plus three more (one for age, sex and education level of the subject) made for a total of fourteen. This total in relation to 120 subjects was well within the Cattell guideline.

The situation was otherwise when only scores of women subjects were analyzed. There were twenty-five different scores plus one for age and one for education—a total of twenty-seven with sixty subjects tested—a ratio of nearly two to one rather than four to one. A total of fifteen scores, including age and education, are all that guideline permits.

Rather than eliminate data *a priori*, a preliminary principal component analysis was carried out on all the data in order that the final analysis include those scores that were seen as most important. This procedure might be criticized by some, but it is thought here that the risk of error in meeting statistical assumptions might be less great than the error of discarding important information.

Men and Women

CORRELATIONS. The eleven performance scores on tests given to both men and women, and the age, sex and education level of the subject, were intercorrelated, providing the matrix seen as Table XVIII. Coefficients of correlation (r) in this table are statistically significant at less than the .01 level when greater than 0.23, and significant at less than the .05 level when greater than 0.17. Of the ninety-one coefficients in Table XVIII, forty-two were 0.23 or greater.

COMPONENTS. The data of Table XVIII were subjected to a principal component analysis. The first four factors, accounting for 62 percent of the variance, were subjected to varimax rotation.[1] Table XIX presents the loading of the fourteen variables on each factor.

The first factor accounted for 26 percent of the variance after rotation, and it appeared to reflect central intactness. Loaded heavily on this factor were the three tests of brain function/perception, the two speed-of-response tasks, and the one of motor control, in terms of slow writing. The tests and their loadings were as follows: VOT (.65), Trailmaking A (.64) and B (.55), Copying Digits (.85), Crossing-Off (.81), and Slow Writing (.42).

Age (−.83) and education (.47) were prominent in this factor. The older the individual, the slower he was—a well-established finding—the more brain function/perception difficulty he appeared to have, and the poorer his motor control (or willingness to reverse a long-established motor habit of writing quickly). Higher education was associated with better performances. The level of education was less prominent on this factor than age and less prominent than it was on factor 4.

It appears, therefore, that both speed-of-response tasks and

---

[1]There are several rules of thumb as to the number of factors to rotate and there is disagreement as to which rule is the best (Rummel, 1970, pp. 359-367). The decision as to the number to rotate in the present study was based on two different rules. Cattell (1966) suggested that the variances of the factors be the determinant. The percentage of accounted-for variance is plotted as a function of the number of the factor and when asymptote is reached, the remaining factors may be regarded as ones of random error. Kaiser (1960) suggested that the decision as to the number of factors be based on the eigenvalues of the factors. If they are less than one, they should not be included in the rotation. In the present chapter, as well as in Chapters 16 and 17, Cattell's guideline was followed, but only when the associated eigenvalues were more than one.

TABLE XVIII

MATRIX OF CORRELATION COEFFICIENTS (r)

(Men and Women Subjects, N = 120)

	1	2	3	4	5	6	7	8	9	10	11	12	13	14
1. Age		.02	—.48	—.59	—.46	—.42	—.62	—.63	—.39	—.27	.04	—.11	—.17	—.25
2. Sex			.03	.24	—.02	—.11	—.07	—.06	—.39	.18	.06	—.09	—.33	—.06
3. Education				.38	.41	.31	.51	.47	.36	.49	—.05	.14	.35	.28
4. VOT (Hooper)					.32	.24	.45	.36	.18	.31	.05	.05	—.05	.19
5. Trailmaking A						.42	.56	.41	.20	.27	—.05	.10	.21	.15
6. Trailmaking B							.43	.32	.30	.22	.08	.22	.16	.23
7. Copying Digits								.77	.40	.29	.02	.10	.23	.20
8. Crossing-Off									.39	.26	.03	.06	.19	.14
9. Slow Writing										.22	—.07	.11	.31	.19
10. Vocabulary											—.03	.02	.15	.20
11. Life Satisfaction												.24	.11	.17
12. Control Rating													.16	.35
13. Clinical Impression														.11
14. Health Rating														

Note: For all tests high scores represent good performances and low scores represent poor performances.

TABLE XIX

ROTATED FACTORS OF PRINCIPAL COMPONENT
ANALYSIS OF DATA IN TABLE XVIII

| Variable | Factors | | | |
	1	2	3	4
Subject Description				
1. Age	—.83	—.03	—.06	—.15
2. Sex	—.02	—.83	—.01	.28
3. Education	.47	.18	.07	.68
Brain Function/Perception				
4. VOT (Hooper)	.65	—.36	.08	.25
5. Trailmaking A	.64	.08	.04	.20
6. Trailmaking B	.55	.17	.30	.05
Psychomotor Speed				
7. Copying Digits	.85	.15	.03	.13
8. Crossing-Off	.81	.14	—.03	.09
9. Slow Writing	.42	.61	—.02	.17
Intelligence				
10. Vocabulary	.20	—.05	.00	.84
Personality/Morale				
11. Life Satisfaction	—.01	—.13	.69	—.15
12. Control Rating	.06	.15	.76	.02
Health/Habit				
13. Clinical Impression	.06	.67	.16	.33
14. Health Rating	.15	.08	.63	.30
Percent Variance	26	13	11	12

simple tests of brain function/perception were part of a common dimension. The two Trailmaking tests might have been expected to load with speed-of-response, since their scores are time scores; however, the VOT (Hooper)—an untimed test—also loaded on this factor. These results lend credence to the contention that the slowing in later life stems from alterations in central nervous system functioning, particularly in terms of information processing. More will be said about this subsequently.

The second factor, which accounted for 13 percent of the variance after rotation, could be labeled a sex factor since sex was represented on this factor by a loading of —.83. It could almost have as meaningfully been labeled a Clinical Impression factor, because also highly loaded on this factor was the examiner's clinical impression of the subjects (.67). The males in the sample appeared more clinically intact to the examiners than did the females; they also performed better on the slow writing test of motor control or habit reversal, the only behavioral measure loading on this factor (.61). (The sex difference in slow writing was discussed in Chapter 4; see Conclusion section in that chapter for interpretation.)

The third factor, which accounted for 11 percent of the variance after rotation, contained three measures with loadings greater than .60—the three self-ratings of health, control over things, and life satisfaction. Since none of the behavioral or subject variables appeared on this factor, it would appear that it reflected a subjective, personal view of one's self, i.e. a tendency to describe one's self consistently in either a positive or negative light. Self-perception of good health was associated with feelings of being in control of life and, in general, feeling content.

The final factor, accounting for 12 percent of the total variance after rotation, might best be labeled a verbal intelligence factor, since the highest loading was that of the WAIS Vocabulary subtest (.84). As to be expected, increased education with a loading of .68 went along with higher intelligence. The next highest loading was Clinical Impression (.33). It is not unreasonable that people with the most verbal facility appear in best mental health to examiners, as well as to others. It is of interest to note that the WAIS Vocabulary score did not load substantially on any of the other three factors, indicating its relative independence from brain function/perception, sex of subject, and the self-rating patterns. Thus, the present results suggest that verbal abilities as measured by the WAIS Vocabulary might be conceptualized as stored information not dependent upon active information processing and, as such, not subject to age-related decline in brain function/perception. [This conclusion is compatible with much of the published literature (as, for example, the summary review of Botwinick, 1967, p. 5-13). However, as will be seen, its generality was brought under question when the present data were analyzed in conjunction with those of memory/learning. This will be discussed in Chapter 17.]

Women

All the variables listed in Table XVII were intercorrelated and subjected to a principal component analysis. However, instead of the Cornell A and Cornell K scores, the more reliable total Cornell measure was used. The resulting rotated factors were then examined for the purpose of selecting fifteen variables which held promise in the subsequent analysis. It will be recalled that only fifteen variables were to be selected in order to fulfill the requirements of Cattell's guideline.

The fifteen variables were selected on the following bases: 1. Age and education were chosen so that the role of these subject variables could be determined in the organization of the varied performances. 2. At least one variable was selected from each of the Chapters 3 through 7, i.e. each of the five categories of behavior. 3. Variables with high loading on the factors were given preference, especially when the high loading was unique to one factor. 4. When two measurements were both highly correlated and intuitively similar in what they measured, one of these was discarded, as necessary. For example, the tasks of Copying Digits and Crossing-Off appear similar, as do Trail-making A and B. 5. When a choice in selecting between two variables was required and no other consideration was apparent, the estimated relative reliabilities was the determiner. The Cornell with many items, for example, was chosen over the Health Self-Rating of only one item.

CORRELATIONS. The 15 variables which were selected may be seen in Table XX, the matrix of correlations. Four variables were selected from each of the categories, Intelligence and Personality/Morale; three variables were chosen from Brain Function/Perception; and one from each of Psychomotor Speed and Health/Habit. Coefficients of correlation in Table XX are significant at the 5 percent level if approximately 0.25 or higher, and significant at the one percent level if approximately .32 or higher. Of the 105 correlation coefficients, 34 were 0.32 or higher.

COMPONENTS. With only sixty women subjects in the study, a principal component analysis may be a questionable procedure to use. Accordingly, special care was taken in interpreting the

TABLE XX

MATRIX OF CORRELATION COEFFICIENTS (r)

(Women Subjects Only, N = 60)

	1	2	3	4	5	6	7	8	9	10	11	12	13	14	15
1. Age		—.24	—.58	—.37	—.40	—.60	—.07	—.15	—.56	—.51	.04	—.16	.33	.35	—.20
2. Education			.13	.17	.24	.24	.25	.45	.35	.39	.03	.00	—.24	—.17	.26
3. VOT (Hooper)				.19	.27	.23	.13	.10	.29	.39	—.07	.08	—.27	—.31	.11
4. Trailmaking B					.40	.23	.14	.19	.37	.20	.05	.13	—.06	—.23	.21
5. Embedded Figure						.20	.25	.29	.55	.54	.14	.20	—.12	—.15	.41
6. Crossing-Off							.09	.07	.33	.36	.07	—.05	—.38	—.37	.06
7. Comprehension								.56	.41	.42	.36	—.08	—.12	—.06	.01
8. Vocabulary									.53	.48	.12	.12	—.13	—.18	.26
9. Block Design										.50	.09	.17	—.13	—.26	.38
10. 16 PF, B-scale											.26	.20	—.34	—.44	.37
11. Control Rating												.38	.15	—.25	.18
12. D-scale													.04	—.48	.48
13. 16 PF, G-scale														.31	.01
14. 16 PF, N-scale															—.23
15. Cornell															

Note: For all tests high scores represent good performances and low scores represent poor performances. Variables Nos. 13 and 14, however, are bipolar in the sense that extreme scores are negative.

results of the analysis by imposing more stringent requirements as to the factor loadings that were considered important. Whereas loadings of .40 and even .30 might be regarded ordinarily as important, in the present analysis, factor loadings less than approximately .50 were not given much attention.

Table XXI shows the results of the principal component analysis based on the correlations seen in Table XXI. The first four factors accounting for 63 percent of the variance were rotated by varimax solution.[2]

The first factor (16 percent of the variance after rotation) was largely one of verbal intelligence. Three measures were prominent: WAIS Vocabulary (.78) and Comprehension (.86), and the 16 PF B-scale (.53). Age (−.03) was not represented on this verbal factor. While this is in accord with much of the published literature—verbal intelligence changes little, if at all, with increasing age—the lack of relationship between age and the B-scale is not in accord. The B-scale is mainly a type of analogy test which does reflect age differences; Chapter 5 shows this as do other reports. Perhaps the relatively low loading (.50 is the cut-off) suggests that much attention not be paid to this variable.

Level of education loaded on this verbal intelligence factor (.52). As may be expected, high education and good verbal ability were associated. This factor appears similar to the fourth factor of Table XIX.

The second rotated factor (18 percent) is not easily understood. As age increased (−.72), performance on the brain function/perception test, VOT (Hooper), decreased (.59), as did speed of Crossing-Off (.74). This much is compatible with the results and conclusions of the principal component analysis based on both men and women (see Table XIX). However, with this pattern, two personality traits appeared, as measured by the 16 PF G- and N-scales. Increased age and decreased performances on the brain function and speed tests were associated with conscientious persevering tendencies (as opposed to

---

[2]The eigenvalue associated with the fifth factor was less than one. See footnote No. 1.

TABLE XXI

ROTATED FACTORS OF PRINCIPAL COMPONENT
ANALYSIS OF DATA IN TABLE XX

Variable	Factors			
	1	*2*	*3*	*4*
Subject Description				
1. Age	—.03	—.72	.00	—.51
2. Education	.52	.23	—.05	.24
Brain Function/Perception				
3. VOT (Hooper)	.01	.59	—.01	.31
4. Trailmaking B	.07	.16	.00	.61
5. Embedded Figure	.28	.13	.09	.72
Psychomotor Speed				
6. Crossing-Off	.10	.74	.02	.10
Intelligence				
7. Comprehension	.86	.02	.05	—.03
8. Vocabulary	.78	.01	.08	.25
9. Block Design	.48	.24	.04	.64
10. 16 PF, B-scale	.53	.47	.30	.33
Personality/Morale				
11. Control Rating	.34	—.12	.72	—.11
12. D-scale	—.15	—.02	.82	.30
13. 16 PF, G-scale	—.17	—.72	.06	.13
14. 16 PF, N-scale	—.03	—.57	—.64	—.07
Health/Habit				
15. Cornell	.06	—.08	.43	.64
Percent Variance	16	18	13	16

expediency and disregard for rules: the G-scale factor loading
was —.72). Moreover, this pattern was associated with the trait
of shrewdness and calculating (as opposed to being forthright
and natural—N-scale, factor loading = —.57). The mix of these
personality and ability measures in association with age was
not anticipated. Perhaps the effort of conscientious and persevering behavior, along with shrewdness and calculation, is
helpful in defending against failing ability in old age.

Table XXI indicates that the third rotated factor (13 percent)
was a personality factor: As depressive affect increased (D-scale,
factor loading = .82) feelings of being in control diminished (.72).
Along with this, the personality trait of being natural and forthright decreased (N-scale, factor loading = —.64). Age was not
associated with this personality complex (.00).

The fourth rotated factor (16 percent) appeared similar to the second, at least as interpretation is concerned; but, instead of speed of response, health was a consideration. As age increased, health decreased (Cornell, .64), and this was associated with poorer brain function/perception test performances (Trailmaking B [.61], Embedded Figures [.72], and Block Design [.64]). This latter test, according to Wechsler (1958, p. 174), is diagnostic of organic brain syndrome. The "organic's inability to do the Block Design test . . . is systematically associated with disturbances in visual-motor organization."

CONCLUSIONS

When the available data of men and women subjects were subjected to a principal component analysis, a rotated first factor was extracted which accounted for 26 percent of the variance. This first factor could be labeled an aging factor; prominently associated with increasing adult age were decreasing performances on tests of brain function/perception and of psychomotor speed. More specifically, associated with age were performances on the VOT (Hooper), Trailmaking A and B, Copying Digits, Crossing-Off, and to a lesser extent, Slow Writing.

It was indicated that the VOT, as an untimed test, might have been expected to load on a different factor, one on which speed and timing were not prominent in good test performances. The fact that all these tests were correlated with the first factor suggested that central intactness, as well as aging, was an appropriate designation of the factor.

Many psychologists would not think of speed-of-response as as integral aspect of brain function. Many might relegate it to mainly motor functioning. Although many measures of perception and cognition have, inherent to them, a speed component, it is typically thought of as part of a peripheral mechanism. The present data suggest, on the contrary, that at least certain speed tasks do measure, or at least are related to, aspects of central intactness. This is in keeping with the position of several investigators—most notably, Birren (1964, p. 111-112)—that age-related behavioral slowness reflects decline in central processing of information.

Later on, in Chapter 17, it will be seen that VOT performances and those of the speed tests (both brain function/perception and psychomotor) were not related, as they were here. While this called for some reformulation of the present interpretation, the additional information in that chapter provided more reason to accept its basic validity.

In the present chapter, when selected test scores of only women subjects were analyzed by the principal component method, two factors were extracted which could be labeled aging factors. One was very similar to the factor described above, but had the additional variable loadings to suggest that as age increased and test performances decreased, persevering and calculating behavior patterns appear, perhaps to maximize performance in the face of expected failure. The other factor also showed the relationship between increasing age and decreasing brain function test performance, but associated with this was decreasing health. The specific tests which related to both the aging factors were the VOT (Hooper), Trailmaking B, Embedded Figures, Block Design, Crossing-Off, Cornell, and the PF scales, G and N.

Thus, brain function/perception, speed of response, health and personality measures were seen to characterize adult aging. Next, we turn to the memory/learning tasks, many of which also characterize adult aging.

Part II

MEMORY/LEARNING

CHAPTER NINE

LONG-TERM MEMORY

It is clinical experience and commonly believed that elderly people recall old memories better than new ones. Some of the older research studies have sought to investigate this belief, as, for example, one of the best ones, that by Shakow, Dolkart and Goldman (1941). They gave people of many different ages the task of recalling old memories (such as personal information, naming objects, alphabet reciting) and also tasks of recalling new information (very recently acquired in the laboratory). Shakow et al. concluded that the loss with age was greater for the recall of the new information than for the old.

There are problems with studies such as these, three of which are especially important :

1. Very obviously, for information to be correctly recalled, it must first be acquired. If there is an age-related difficulty in acquiring information, if the information is not completely registered (in memory), then comparing old and new recall may be comparing the different processes, recall and acquisition. If so, it would be incorrect to state, as implied in the first sentence of this chapter, that recall is better for memories long in storage than for those only recently in storage. Recall here is synonomous with the retrieval of information that is already acquired.

2. Not all items of information are meaningfully measured by a common scale. Shakow et al. compared old and new memory in terms of a recall score:

> But what does it mean . . . that the old and young subjects are fifteen units apart in remembering names (old memories) and twenty-five units apart in remembering new acquired digits (new memories)? There is no common base on which to compare the difficulty, meaningfulness, and other characteristics of the stimulus materials (Botwinick, 1967, p. 116-117).

81

3. In saying that there is not a common base on which to compare the meaningfulness of the information, it is suggested that important memories, ones that are long held and frequently referred to (rehearsed often), memories that have impact on our lives, are retained better than those that are not. This is not quite the same as saying that it is the age of the material in storage that determines how good recall will be in later life.

The present study is of old versus more recent memory in relation to age and it avoids some of the problems above. These will be discussed after the presentation of the results.

PROCEDURE

Each subject was asked twenty-four questions of specific information. There were six questions referring to each of four time periods in which historic events occurred. There were six questions in each of the periods, 1950-1969, 1930-1949, 1910-1929, and 1890-1909.

The twenty-four questions may be seen in Appendix C. Two examples, however, will be given here: from the most recent period, "In what city was President John F. Kennedy assassinated?"; and from the oldest period, "What was the name of the man who became president when President McKinley was assassinated in 1900?"

The data were collected during the period December 1969 to spring 1971, with most of it collected in the year 1970. If the four historic periods are roughly categorized as 1960, 1940, 1920 and 1900, and the subjects of the study roughly twenty-five, thirty-five, forty-five, fifty-five, sixty-five, and seventy-five years when tested, the relative recency-remoteness of the information could be calculated.[1]

----

[1]For example, if the subjects were born during the years 1945, 1935, 1925, 1915, 1905 and 1895, then it may be calculated that the oldest subjects were young adults (twenty-five years) when events in the 1920 period occurred, middle age (forty-five years) when the 1940 events occurred, and sixty-five years of age when the most recent events occurred. The youngest subjects were approximately fifteen years old when the most recent events occurred and not yet born when did the other events. None of the subjects were adult when the most remote events took place.

RESULTS

There were four historic time periods from which subjects within the six age groups were asked for the recall of information. By means of an analysis of variance, the age groups were tested for differences in overall recall and for recall as it related to the historic time periods (the interaction between Age and Period in Table XXII).

TABLE XXII

ANALYSIS OF VARIANCE OF RECALL SCORES RELATED
TO FOUR HISTORICAL TIME PERIODS

Source	df	MS	F
Between Subjects	119		
Educ. (E)	1	41.21	8.06‡
Sex (S)	1	156.55	30.61†
Age (A)	5	5.33	1.04
A X S	5	7.36	1.44
Residual	107	5.11	
Within Subjects	360		
Period (P)	3	41.16	41.58†
E X P	3	1.14	1.15
S X P	3	3.15	3.18§
A X P	15	2.40	2.42‡
A X S X P	15	0.87	0.88
Residual	321	0.99	
Total	479		

† $p < .0001$
‡ $p < .01$
§ $p < .05$

The statistical test that was made in comparing age groups was a very conservative one. Age differences in recall were adjusted for by the effect that level of education, and the sex of the subject, has on recall performances.[2]

Table XXII shows that the age groups were not significantly different in their ability to provide the information ($p > .05$). A less conservative, more traditional test was made by which age effects were not adjusted for education and sex differences.

---

[2]The test for age differences was made by a step-down, nonorthogonal hierarchical design, in the manner described in Chapter 2, section on Data Analysis and Presentation.

Again, the results showed that age was not a significant factor in how much information was recalled ($p > .05$).

Table XXII discloses that the two sexes were significantly different in their recall performances ($p < .0001$): Men were very much better at recall than women. (See Figure 8 showing means of the measured performances.) Education was also a factor in recall ($p < .01$); those subjects with more than twelve years of formal schooling performed better than those with twelve or less years.

Table XXII also shows that the information of the four historic time periods was not recalled equally. The source of variation, Period, was statistically significant at less than the .0001 level: there was better recall for the more recent information than for the older information. The mean recall scores for the information of the periods 1950 to 1969, 1930 to 1949, 1910 to 1929, and 1890 to 1909 were, respectively, 3.00, 3.05, 2.61, and 1.78. It is to be noted that the range of possible scores for each of these time periods was zero through 6.

The most important source of variation in Table XXII, from the point of view of testing the hypothesis that age deficits in memory are related to how long the memories have been in storage, is the interaction between Age and Period (A X P). This interaction was statistically significant at less than the .01 level. Despite this statistical significance, however, examination of Figure 8 disclosed a complexity which denied precise and total support of the hypothesis, although partial support was seen.

Figure 8 shows that the decline with age was relatively sharp when information of the 1950's and 1960's was recalled; on the other hand, the decline was minimal, if at all present, when information of the 1910's and 1920's was recalled. For events occurring during the 1930's and 1940's, recall seemed to *increase* up to middle age and then decline. Events of the 1890's to 1909 were unexperienced history for nearly all the subjects, and for neither men nor women was there a clear aging pattern in recall. Estimated means by age groups (accounting for unequal subclass size) may be seen in Table XXIII.

The approximate ages of the subjects at the time the to-be-recalled event took place is given in Figure 8. For example,

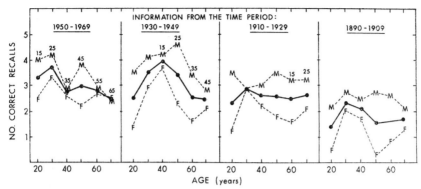

Figure 8. Mean correct recalls as a function of age, sex, and historical time period. Dashed lines represent men (M) and women (F). Numbers in graphs represent approximate mean ages of the subjects at the time the historical event took place.

subjects aged in their fifties at the time of testing were twenty-five when events of the 1930's and 1940's took place. It may be seen in Figure 8 and Table XXIII that, in a most general way, peak recall performances were for those events that took place when the subjects were approximately fifteen to twenty-five years of age.

Table XXII shows that the interaction between the sex of subject and the time period was significant at less than the .05 level. Since very many statistical tests were made in the total study described in this book, a more stringent criterion than the 5 percent level is thought necessary for accepting differences as significant. Thus, not too much is to be made of this interaction between sex and time period. What trend may be indicated

TABLE XXIII

LONG-TERM MEMORY: ESTIMATED PERFORMANCE
MEANS BY AGE DECADES

Historical Time Period	Age ((Years)					
	20s	*30s*	*40s*	*50s*	*60s*	*70s*
1890-1909	1.36	2.37	2.11	1.50	1.68	1.69
1910-1929	2.25	2.72	2.60	2.67	2.52	2.71
1930-1949	2.37	3.36	3.87	3.47	2.60	2.50
1950-1969	3.18	3.62	2.68	3.02	2.89	2.50

by this interaction is that the two sexes were more similar in recall with the most recent information than with the others.

CONCLUSIONS

The present study tested the hypothesis that increasing age is associated with long-term recall such that memories long in storage are increasingly better remembered than memories that are of more recent year. As indicated, the results of the present study supported the hypothesis to an extent only. There was no age decline in the recall of long-term memory; this finding is a surprise in view of all the reports in the literature stating clearly that memory ability declines with age. Perhaps the reason that overall age differences were not found here is that memories of various ages were tested. For example, Figure 8 shows that subjects aged seventy to seventy-nine years recalled information from the 1910's and 1920's about as well as anyone else, but some decline with age was seen with memories of the more recent era, 1950's and 1960's. If the finding of no age difference is attributed to the fact that memories of various ages were tested, then partial support of the hypothesis is implicit.

The test of the hypothesis and the conclusion of this study rest on three assumptions discussed early in the chapter. There is no problem with one of these assumptions, but there is with at least one other. First, the assumption without problems is that to compare memories of different age it is necessary to have a common scale of measurement—one that is assumed as appropriate for old memories as for newer ones. Since in the present study all the information, being historical events, has a similar character, no such problem is seen with this assumption.

A second assumption is that the amount of information acquired, i.e. the amount of information in memory, is the same for all age groups. This assumption permits the measurement of recall rather than the measurement of acquired knowledge. This assumption may be tenable to the extent that the asked-for information is generally available to all, is impersonal, and is similar in type from time period to time period. This assumption may not be correct, however, if a third one is untenable, i.e.

the old and newer memories are of equal importance to people within the different age groups. If information of one era is more relevant to people of one age than information of another era, the two sets of information may not have equal probability of being registered in memory.

Information of the assassination of President Kennedy may be of greater importance to the forty-year-old than information of the assassination of President McKinley. The forty-year-old may have known about McKinley before Kennedy, i.e. the McKinley memory was the older one, but the new information had more relevance. There is evidence in Figure 8 and Table XXIII that something like this may be operating. It was pointed out that peak performances were made by subjects who were fifteen to twenty-five years old at the time the historic event took place. For those aged thirty-five when the event occurred, recall did not seem nearly as good. When no person was yet adult to experience the event (from the 1890's to 1909), there was no special decline with age. In this latter situation, it is likely that the older subjects acquired the information before the young subjects did—they had it in memory longer. If it was simply a matter of the age of the memory, the older subjects should have shown better recall than the younger ones. It is interesting to note that, in Figure 8 and Table XXIII, the youngest subjects, those in their twenties and not yet alive when most of the events occurred, performed poorly. They were at their relative best, however, with the information acquired at approximately age fifteen.

If it is impact or importance of the memory more than its age that determines recall, then the first sentence of this chapter—clinical experience and common belief have it that elderly people recall old memories better than new ones—refers to hardly anything more amazing than that the older memories better recalled are those that were important in the first place, having had some impact on life. How many old memories that are not important are forgotten? Perhaps it is both the importance of the memory and its age that make for good recall.

Whatever the important variable or variables in the present study may be, they seemed more true for men than women. It did not come as a surprise that those more highly educated recalled more information than those of lower education. But it certainly was not expected that men would be so much better than women in the recall of the information. Table XXII shows that the largest mean square, by far, was that associated with the sex of the subject. Perhaps the information asked of the subjects was more appropriate to men than women, although this was neither intended nor even considered as a possibility beforehand.

The sizable differences in recall between the sexes were seen in every age group. It was also seen with teenagers and young college students in data not reported here. If these results are not due to the greater appropriateness of the test information for men than women, the results speak to the opportunities, demands, or responsibilities in learning and knowing that have not been presented to women. For this or other reasons, the conclusions of the present study and the generalizations that were made are more appropriate for men than women.

CHAPTER TEN

MEMORY FOR SPANS AND
SEQUENTIAL PATTERNS

F OR INFORMATION AND experience to become part of the person, so to speak, for them to be stored in a memory bank and available for later recall, they must first be impressed or registered in the nervous system and filed away. What is filed is called an engram or a memory trace.

In the previous chapter, investigation was made of old memory traces. Obviously, before traces become old they must first be new. New trace formation is examined in the next chapter and in others that follow; in the present chapter, a type of memory is investigated which could be conceptualized as one that may not involve the trace registration process and the engram. It could be conceptualized as a more fleeting type of memory, a memory that is just passed through the nervous system.

There is a controversy whether once traces are formed they decay on their own or whether forgetting is to be attributed to interference by competing events. Without getting into this controversy, it seems clear that with memories of such short duration, thought to simply pass through—memories that are a few seconds or less in duration—interference may not be the complete or best explanation for the forgetting. Examples of this are the perceptual (P) system of Broadbent (1958), or the primary memory (PM) of Waugh and Norman (1965), or even, possibly the primary stimulus trace of Sperling (1960).

In the present study very short-duration recall, which is related to some of the above, was studied: it is memory for spans and patterns. This type of memory is sometimes experienced in telephone dialing. A seven-digit phone number is retained just long enough to complete the dialing, but if the dialing is interrupted it may be necessary to look up the number again. It is as if the span of seven digits is not registered in memory; it is held only long enough for the dialing; it is as if the information is just passed through. The present chapter deals with such short-term recall, leaving it open whether or not registration is to be emphasized more than passing through.

In addition to this type of recall as it relates to age, the present chapter includes an investigation of the sensory modality by which the information is experienced. It also includes investigation of the type of information that is experienced as it relates to recall. Does the specific sense modality make a difference as to the extent age groups differ in their memory spans? Does the type of content information make a difference?

PROCEDURES

Nine span tasks, given to both men and women subjects, constituted the procedures of this chapter. The tasks can be divided into two groupings of six and three each. In the larger group there were digit and letter sequences to be recalled; in the smaller group there were sequential patterns with seemingly less cognitive content; they were more akin to rhythms.

The digits were presented both visually and auditorily, the letters were presented only auditorily. In these procedures, the subjects were asked to recall the items both forward (in the same manner presented by the investigator) and backward (in the opposite order). There were thus these tasks: auditory digits, forward and backward; auditory letters, forward and backward; visual digits, forward and backward. (The backward recall does not fit the passing through hypothesis without further stipulation. One is suggested later.)

The patterns related to three sense modalities: visual, auditory, and kinesthetic. Patterns were recalled only in the forward fashion.

Digit and Letter Span

The investigator, in the auditory digit task said to the subject,

"I am going to read you some numbers. When I finish I want you to say them back to me. For example, if I say 6, 2, 7, you would say............?" The investigator then proceeded to present each subject with a graded series of digits beginning with three in each series and ending with eight in each series. (If the subject had difficulty with the instructions, the first series would be only two in length.)

There were two different series in each length; the second was presented only if the first was not recalled perfectly. For example, the shortest span length given was 8, 5, 2 and then 5, 9, 4 if the first was not recalled. Each digit was read to the subject at the approximate rate of one per second.

The auditory letters spans were presented in similar fashion. As an example, the three-letter sequences were: Z, K, A and W, M, Y; the first of the eight-letter sequence was B, R, X, M, A, U, W, H.

The backward version of these span tests was introduced to the subjects with these instructions: "I am going to read to you some more numbers but this time when I stop I want you to say the numbers (letters) backward. For example if I say 7, 2, 4 (L, G, S), you would say...............?" The backward span test was given immediately following the forward span test of the same type. The scores for both the forward and the backward tests were the longest series of items perfectly recalled in perfect order, with one of the two presentations. When both the two trials were not recalled perfectly, the span test was terminated.

The visual digits task was similar to the auditory tasks except for one important difference. Instead of each digit being presented one at a time, the series was presented on a card, at once. For example, the three-digit series was presented on a single card and read 7, 6, 1. Differences in recall between auditory and visual digits, therefore, could be a function of either (or both) the sense modality and the whole stimulus presentation in the case of visual stimulation and item-by-item in the case of auditory stimulation.

Pattern Recall

The test format of pattern recall was designed to be similar to that of the auditory span tests except that backward tests were not given.

VISION. In the visual test, four small blocks of wood were placed in a row, two inches apart. With the examiner sitting opposite the subject, the blocks may be designated 4, 3, 2 and 1 going from the subject's right to left. The examiner instructed the subject: "I am going to point to these blocks one after another. Watch carefully. When I finish I want you to point to the blocks in the same order in which I did. For example, if I point (pointing to 4 and then 2), you would then point to which ones?"

As in the spans tests, two series were given for each length of pattern, with three items (pointings to the blocks) the shortest length given and six items the longest length. As an example, the first three-item test was 1, 4, 3, referring to block placement positions. The score was the longest series perfectly recalled (by pointing).

AUDITION. The auditory pattern test had these instructions to the subject: "We are going to do something very similar. But this time instead of pointing to the blocks I am going to knock on the table in a kind of code. Listen carefully. When I finish I'm going to ask you to repeat the code by knocking on the table just like I did. For example, if I knock like this (one knock, pause, two knocks) what would you do?" (The pause between knocks was just long enough to break the rhythmic chain, i.e. the unit-item sound.)

If the subject correctly reproduced the auditory pattern the test began with a two-item series. The simplest task was 2, 2 (two knocks, pause, two knocks). The first pattern of six items—the longest pattern—was 1, 2, 1, 3, 2, 3. None of the series lengths included an item greater than three knocks. As in the other procedures, the test was terminated with two failures on a particular series length.

KINESTHESIS. The kinesthetic pattern test was very similar to the auditory one. "We are going to do something similar to what we just finished. Instead of knocking on the table I'm going to touch the back of your hand. . . . When I finish I want you to touch my hand (in response). For example, I touch your hand like this (pressing the forefinger on back of subject's hand once, pause, then pressing twice). Now you do the same thing to me."

The test began with the pattern 2, 1 (two presses, pause, one press). Level six, the longest pattern, was 3, 2, 1, 2, 3, 1. Again, no item in the pattern was more frequent than three presses.

RESULTS

A multivariate analysis of variance was carried out on the performance scores based upon the nine tests of recall, i.e. Spans (visual-auditory, digits-letters, forward-backward) and Patterns (visual, auditory, kinesthetic). The six age groups were found significantly different in their performances ($p < .025$), as were the two education groups ($p < .001$), i.e. those with more than twelve years of formal schooling and those with twelve or less years. Sex differences were not statistically significant ($p < .05$).

Education was ordered first, and age last, in this step-down hierarchical design (see Chapter 2, section on Data Analysis and Presentation). These significant results permitted univariate and other analyses.

Spans and Patterns

The span and pattern procedures are very similar. As indicated, except for the backward recall tasks, it would seem that the major difference between them is the larger role that cognitive content plays in spans. Digits and letters are obvious aspects of prior learning; patterns and rhythms may not involve cognitive content at all unless the subjects attempt to count the pattern items rather than reproduce them by other means.

The apparent similarity in forward recall of the span and pattern procedures seemed to justify analyzing them together. An analysis of variance was performed in which performances on each task were given maximum scores of 6, enabling comparisons among the six forward recall procedures.

Table XXIV shows the results of this analysis. Age differences

TABLE XXIV

ANALYSIS OF VARIANCE OF SPAN AND PATTERN FORWARD RECALL

Source	df	MS	F
Between Subjects	119		
Educ. (E)	1	9.25	9.67§
Sex (S)	1	0.04	0.04
Age (A)	5	4.98	5.21‡
A X S	5	0.75	0.78
Residual	107	0.96	
Within Subjects	600		
Tasks (T)	5	97.13	231.26†
E X T	5	1.85	4.40§
S X T	5	0.65	1.54
A X T	25	0.65	1.54
A X S X T	25	0.37	0.88
Residual	535	0.42	
Total	719		

† $p < .0001$
‡ $p < .001$
§ $p < .01$

were statistically significant ($p < .001$), as were education group differences ($p < .01$). The latter, however, were not significant ($p > .05$) when ordered last and therefore adjusted for age and sex effects. The magnitude and nature of these differences will be discussed when presenting the results of the univariate analyses.

Table XXIV shows no significant interaction between age and the six recall procedures ($p > .05$). This suggests that whatever may be the difference in recall performance between young and old adults, it is similar for all the tasks. This conclusion is limited, however, to the score of 6 as the highest possible with each task. Had the difficulty level been extended beyond six items in all the tasks, the interaction might have been otherwise, although this does not seem indicated by the data in Table XXV and Figure 9. These are mean scores based upon possible top scores of 8 with the span tasks.

PATTERNS. When the three pattern tasks (auditory, visual and kinesthetic) were examined separately from the others, a similar result was found, i.e. statistically significant age and

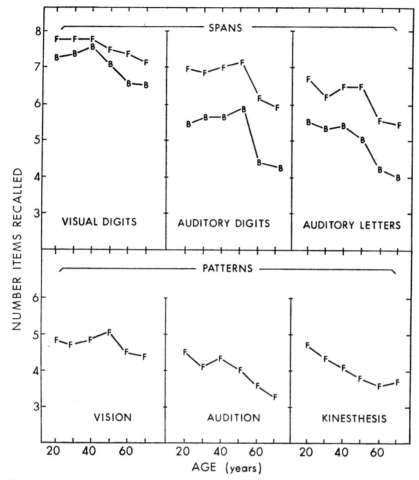

Figure 9. Maximum number of items recalled as a function of age. The highest possible score in span recall was 8; the highest in pattern recall was 6. (F = forward recall, B = backward recall).

education differences, but no significant age pattern with respect to the sense modality that was stimulated. Recall was best with visual stimulation (overall estimated mean of 4.72), next with kinesthetic (4.04), and last with auditory (3.98), but this sense modality pattern was similar for the six age groups. (It is assumed that these three mean scores, and the others in this study, are not influenced appreciably by the order in which the tests were administered—see Appendix A.)

SPANS. As indicated, recall was so measured with the six span tasks that a possible top score on each task was 8, not 6, as in the analysis of Table XXIV. An analysis of variance was carried out with the recall scores, which included both forward and backward recall. The analysis was a very long one, too long to present in detail for the items of information that are most important here. (The analysis included nineteen sources of variation, not counting the four error terms, the total between and total within subject variations, or the grand total.)

The items of central interest may be put in three questions referring to three sources of interaction variation: 1. Does the type of span task (auditory, visual, digits, letters) make a difference with respect to aging? (That is, is the interaction between age and span type statistically significant?) 2. Does recall order (forward versus backward) make a difference with respect to aging? (Is the interaction between age and order statistically significant?) It seems reasonable that backward recall would more likely involve registration and trace formation than forward recall. Perhaps this is a crucial factor in aging memory. 3. Does the combination of span type and order of recall make a difference in aging? (Is the interaction of age, span type, and order statistically significant?)

Based on the results of the analysis, questions 2 and 3 above are easily answered in the negative. While there was a significant difference among the three types of span tests ($p < .0001$) and between whether the recall was forward or backward ($p < .0001$), neither of these variables in conjunction with age contributed significantly to the performance variance ($p > .05$). Neither was the interaction between age and order statistically significant ($p > .05$). The overall recall performances were best with the visual task (estimated means = 7.34), next with auditory digits (6.00), and last with auditory letters (5.53). Forward recall was superior to backward recall.

The first question must be answered more equivocally, but perhaps with a leaning to the negative. The interaction between age and type of span test was marginally significant ($p < .05$) when age was ordered last in the step-down analysis, i.e. when age effects were adjusted for education and sex differences.

TABLE XXV

MEMORY FOR SPANS AND PATTERNS: ESTIMATED
PERFORMANCE MEANS BY AGE DECADES

Tests*	Age (Years)					
	20s	*30s*	*40s*	*50s*	*60s*	*70s*
ADF	7.08	7.05	7.13	7.13	6.10	5.90
ADB	5.41	5.53	5.61	6.00	4.51	4.36
ALF	6.70	6.20	6.50	6.50	5.50	5.45
ALB	5.41	5.18	5.31	5.07	4.31	4.06
VDF	7.76	7.72	7.76	7.51	7.45	7.18
VDB	7.38	7.54	7.68	7.08	6.45	6.60
AP	4.53	4.11	4.33	4.00	3.62	3.26
VP	4.86	4.73	4.86	5.05	4.48	4.39
KP	4.63	4.22	4.03	3.82	3.69	3.74

* Test descriptions: A = auditory, V = visual, K = kinesthetic; D = digits, L = letters, P = patterns; F = forward, B = backward recall. Highest possible mean score of each span text (first six) is 8; highest of each Pattern Test (last three) is 6.

However, when age effects were not so adjusted, when age was ordered first, the interaction between age and type of span test was significant at less than the one percent level. Thus, what differential role the type of span test plays in regard to age is at least partly a function of education level. An examination of the span data in Table XXV suggests that if there is a differential age effect in terms of the types of tasks, it is small indeed.

Univariate Analyses

An analysis of variance was carried out for each of the nine procedures (see Table XXVI). The overall result suggested an association between age and memory for spans and patterns, but one that is not especially great. Despite levels of statistical significance in six of the nine variance analyses, none of the F-ratios associated with age were large, and as determined by ω^2 analyses, the percent of performance variance accounted for by age did not exceed 13 in any of them; two of the significant six were as low as 7 percent.

The analyses in Table XXVI were carried out with age effects adjusted for education and sex differences. Two of the three analyses in which age effects were not statistically significant became so ($p < .01$) when age was ordered first in the step-down design, i.e. when age was not adjusted for the effects of education and sex differences. Only visual pattern recall showed

TABLE XXVI

ANALYSES OF VARIANCES OF SPANS AND PATTERNS TEST SCORES

Source	df	Span Tests*						Pattern Tests*		
		ADF	ADB	ALF	ALB	VDF	VDB	AP	VP	KP
Educ. (E)	1	1.39	14.83†	7.41‡	19.59†	9.47‡	1.98	7.11‡	0.20	11.83†
Sex (S)	1	0.23	0.04	0.02	2.13	0.02	1.18	0.61	0.69	1.71
Age (A)	5	3.87‡	4.85†	4.92†	3.15§	1.75	2.88§	4.34‡	1.75	2.12
A X S	5	1.81	1.12	3.23‡	1.01	0.64	1.05	0.21	1.77	0.54
Residual**	107	1.25	1.46	0.93	1.44	0.46	1.13	0.83	0.65	0.95
Total	119									

* Test descriptions: A = auditory, V = visual, K = kinesthetic; D = digits, L = letters, P = patterns; F = forward, B = backward recall.

** Residuals are represented by mean squares. All other sources of variation are represented by F-ratios.

† $p < .001$ to $< .0001$

‡ $p < .01$

§ $p < .02$

no age effect when age was ordered first. The general pattern was for a decline in recall performance with increased age, as seen by the estimated means in Table XXV and by the observed means in Figure 9.

Table XXVI also shows that education groups were significantly different in six of the nine tests ($p < .01$ to $< .0001$). However, when education effects were adjusted for those of age and sex, only one test showed significance and that of only less than the .04 level. Thus, education level did not appear to be an important factor in the type of recall measured by these tests. Sex differences were not observed with any of the nine procedures ($p > .05$).

Overall then, these results indicated a statistically significant but low order relationship between age and recall. Even lower in order were the education level and the sex of the subject. Neither the sense modality stimulated, nor the type of task given, made a difference in regard to age patterns in recall performances.

CONCLUSIONS

Memory for spans and patterns as measured here was thought to reflect a minimum role for memory storage, and perhaps a minimum role for memory registration as well. It was thought to reflect, at least in part, a passing through of information, i.e. a perceptual intake and almost immediate expression (response) of it. This would require little mental organization of the input, except in the case of the backward recalls. Even the backward recalls, however, could be conceptualized in the passing through model: the perceptual intake is held only long enough to permit a read-out in reverse. The holding may be thought of as something short of true registration.

This very short-term holding of information is similar to the conceptualization Kay (1968) discussed for digits recalled in forward fashion. Kay made a distinction among three varieties of short-term memory. First there is the passing through of information, the primary stimulus trace (Sperling, 1960). For Kay, this is essentially a phenomenon of the "peripheral sensory system." Second, there is "something more central . . . information has been received, and in many instances perceived . . . there is little or no time for rehearsal of the (memory span) series. . . ." Third, "material is both perceived and deliberately rehearsed (registered). This happens in some digit span experiments where the rate of presentation is not too fast." (Kay, 1968, p. 67)

It would seem that Kay's second category would find much of the span and pattern memory data of the present study. However, regardless of whether the data would best be conceptualized in this way or by the concept of passing through, performances were only minimally related to age, although the relation was statistically significant.

There were several experimental variations of the nine procedures that might have indicated areas of strength and weakness the elderly have in recall performance. There were variations in the sensory modality stimulated and in the types of information to be recalled. None of the experimental variations indicated differential memory ability with age, only an overall lower level of performance.

In the main, these results are compatible with much of the recent literature. Talland (1968, p. 125) conducted a series of studies of forward memory span in relation to age and concluded that the "human capacity to transmit information diminishes with advancing age. . . ." A perusal of his data suggested, however, that he too found the age effect a relatively small one. Bromley (1958) found no significant difference in span recall among three groups of mean age twenty-seven, forty-six, and sixty-six years; Gilbert (1941) reported only an 8 percent decline by age sixty.

Talland had several variations in his experimental procedures; although he concluded from his results that age decrements in recall were greater "under some conditions than under others" (p. 126), overall, as in the present study, relatively little interaction between age and the experimental manipulations were seen. Of important note, whereas McGhie, Chapman, and Lawson (1965) reported that visual digit span declines more with age than does auditory span, this was found neither by Talland nor here.

Another type of experimental variation was conducted by Taub (1973). He examined the effect of repeated testing sessions with the finding that they provided greater benefit for the young than the old. Kinsbourne (1973) varied the speed with which item letters were auditorily presented. Span recall was less good on the part of the elderly subjects than younger ones but of more importance; the fast presentation speed he used hindered the performances of the elderly subjects, but not the young ones. Kinsbourne concluded that "Old people are disproportionately handicapped by the need for rapid registration of incoming information. . . ." Perhaps in implicit recognition that registration may not be the key to understanding span recall, he also suggested that the registration phenomenon may be preceded by "an age-related exacerbation on the normal limitations on perception of rapidly sequential messages" (p. 319).

The present investigation together with those briefly reviewed here emphasize three main results: 1. Whether the basic mechanism of memory for spans and patterns is that of registration or of passing through, there is a decline of this type of memory with age. 2. The decline, however, is not great, and if measured with only short span lists, it may not be manifest at all. Further, the percent of recall performance that was accounted for by age ranged from only 7 to 13, as measured in the present study. 3. None of the present experimental manipulations and very few in the reported literature seemed to differentially benefit the elderly. An exception might be slow experimental pacing.

A procedure of very slow stimulus pacing would maximize the need for memory registration; it would not allow for a sensory passing through of information which must be reasonably rapid. Slow experimental pacing differentially benefiting the elderly suggests that they might do better in recall that clearly and obviously requires registration than that which does not, as perhaps, that in spans and patterns. However, the next chapter deals with memory registration, and it will be seen that within the stimulus pacing schedules used, the elderly had great difficulty. This fact may speak to a passing through dimension of span and pattern memory.

CHAPTER ELEVEN

SHORT-TERM AND DELAYED RECALL
OF ROTE LEARNING

THE NOTION THAT memory ability declines with age is often based upon clinical and laboratory investigations of a type of memory which is indistinguishable from a type of learning. It is all the more paradoxical, therefore, that many people seem quite comfortable complaining, "I have a poor memory," but uncomfortable with the idea, "I don't learn well."

The present chapter deals with this type of memory/learning. It is of short-term memory, clearly involving registration. Unlike the data of Chapter 9 (Long-term Memory), where learning was assumed to have taken place long age and outside the laboratory; and unlike the data of Chapter 10 (Memory for Spans and Sequential Patterns), where the idea was entertained that much of what was recalled had hardly been registered (learned) at all, but possibly, instead, just perceived and passed-through; the present chapter deals with obvious learning in the laboratory and recall very shortly thereafter. There is a controversy whether this type of memory/learning declines with age, which will be discussed briefly toward the end of the chapter.

The two procedures used here to measure short-term recall are classic ones for psychologists; they are paired-associate learning and serial learning. The present chapter also examines delayed recall of what had been learned and recalled earlier.

PROCEDURES

There were three paired-associate tasks and two serial learning tasks, each with eight items to be learned. Four of the five tasks were given a second time to measure delayed recall. Nine separate testings, therefore, were given to each male and female subject. The delayed recall procedures were given to the subject after completing the initial recall task and experiencing three other procedures of the test battery (see Appendix A).

Paired-Associates

The first two paired-associate tasks were similar except for one important difference—their difficulty. The instructions to the subject were as follows: "I am going to read you a list of eight pairs of words. . . . After I finish reading the list, I will ask you to tell me what words go together. For example, if the words I read are Salty—Sweet, Joy—Happy, when I say Salty you would say (Sweet). When I say Joy you would say (Happy).

The eight pairs were: ocean—water, dream—sleep, eagle—bird, hand—foot, blue—sky, Woman—man, dark—light, stomach—food.

It can be observed that the pairs go together; there is a high association between them. Water goes with ocean and food goes with stomach. The second paired-associate test was different only in that teh words did not go together in this way; there is a lower association between them. The second paired-associate list was: table—music, book—hair, king—stem, moon—thief, circle —baby, river—stove, sheep—hammer, bread—carpet.

Both these lists were given such that five seconds were allowed for response after the stimulus word (the first word of the pair) was presented. If the subject failed to respond or gave a wrong response associate, the investigator supplied the correct one.

Each complete list was given ten times or to the criterion of three perfect trials, whichever came first. The three perfect trials did not have to be consecutive. (A perfect trial is one in which the subject responds with the correct associate to each of eight stimulus items.) Each time the list was presented, it was given with a different ordering of the paired associates.

The third paired-associate list was different from the first two in that instead of a stimulus word there was a stimulus of two consonants. The eight-item list was RW—sugar, FP—wagon, BK—tiger, NT—cover, HD—medal, YS—honey, GL—satin, XM—paper.

The list was given in the same way as the other two. The score for each list was based on the number of trials to criterion.

For the purpose of ease in relating the scores to other data, to have a high score represent good performance, the trials to criterion were subtracted from eleven. Thus, if the third perfect trial was the ninth one, the subject would get a score of 2 (11 − 9). If the third perfect trial was the fifth, the score would be 6; if three perfect trials were not achieved in ten list presentations, the score would be zero.

Serial Learning

The two serial learning tasks were different from each other mainly in the nature of the recall that was required. In the first task, the recall had to be made in the exact order of the items in the list as given. In the second task, any order of correct items was acceptable—it was a free recall.

The instructions and list of the first task were "I am going to read you a list of eight words. I want you to remember the words in order. Listen carefully. We'll go through the list several times until you get it right." The words, read to the subject at the rate of one per second, were: boxer, salad, razor, panel, magic, lemon, hotel, color. The second, free recall list was: camel, fiber, petal, motor, label, bacon, delay, siren.

Each of the three paired-associate lists and the first of the two serial learning lists were given later at a second time to measure what had been retained after a period of delay and intervening memory test-taking.

RESULTS

The intent was to compare the six age groups, not only with respect to overall recall of the rote learning, i.e. performance on the three paired-associate and two serial learning procedures, but to compare them in relation to differential performance among selected procedures. For example, the intent was, not only to carry out a multivariate analysis of variance including the five procedures, but to carry out a series of variance analyses of selected procedures to determine whether one or more of the task types was relatively easier for one of the age groups or another.

However, so many of the older subjects could not and would not do the more difficult tasks, particularly the paired-associate tasks, that many cases were missed. The tasks were so difficult and seemingly threatening to many subjects, particularly the older ones, that the examiner frequently made the decision to forego testing, to not even try these procedures, in order to minimize a break in the cooperation typical of the subjects of this study. There was fear that the subjects, if pressed too hard, would quit. Because of this, the cell frequencies were too small to carry out all the intended analyses. Thus, those analyses that were carried out took a different form from those in the other chapters of this book.

Paired Associates

THE FIRST PAIRED-ASSOCIATE TASK. The easy task presented no special problem for any age group; in fact, there was no significant difference among the six age groups in their recall performances ($p > .05$). This was so whether age comparisons were made adjusting for education and sex effects or not. Each of the six age groups performed in such a way that their respective mean scores were between 7 and 8, indicating that the third perfect trial occurred between the third and fourth list presentation.

Education level was not an important factor in recall, if it was one at all. Education group differences were not statistically significant when adjustments for age and sex were made ($p > .05$). When the adjustments were not made, differences were significant ($p < .01$), with the more highly educated group performing better . The sex of the subject was not a factor in recall ($p > .05$).

THE SECOND AND THIRD PAIRED-ASSOCIATE TASKS. It has already been indicated that two of the paired-associate tasks were very hard for many of the subjects, particularly the older ones. Table XXVII shows the percent of subjects in each age decade who were given the various tasks and who were able to achieve scores greater than zero. It may be seen in Table XXVII that, among subjects aged in the fifties, only 30 to 35 percent were given the second and third paired-associates test and were able to achieve a score of 1 or better. The percentages of subjects in their seventh and eighth age decades were even lower. Chi square tests of the relationship between age and task completion were carried out for each of the five procedures in Table XXVII, and, except for the first paired-associate test, statistical significance was found at less than the .001 level in each. The chi square tests and Table XXVII show very clearly that taking these tests and performing well on them became progressively less likely as age increased.

TABLE XXVII

PERCENT OF SUBJECTS TESTED AND WITH SCORES
LARGER THAN ZERO

Task*	*Age (Years)*					
	20s	*30s*	*40s*	*50s*	*60s*	*70s*
PA-1	100	100	100	100	100	100
PA-2	90	80	75	35	25	20
PA-3	65	55	75	30	05	0
SL-1	95	100	100	80	80	40
SL-2	95	100	90	70	70	50

* Task Descriptions: PA-1 = easy paired-associates task, both stimulus and response associates were meaningful words; PA-2 = difficult paired-associates task similar to PA-1; PA-3 = difficult paired-associate task, stimuli were two-letter consonants and response associates were meaningful words; SL-1 = serial learning task of ordered recall; SL-2 = serial learning task of free recall.

Separate univariate analyses of variances were carried out with the recall scores of each of the procedures, not including those of subjects who refused to do the tasks or to whom they were not given. The analyses did include, however, performances of those who carried out the task but who did not achieve scores better than zero. In light of the number of subjects in each age decade who were not given or who did not complete the tasks, it is evident that these univariate analyses underestimate the extent of age differences.

With both the second and the third paired-associates tasks, the age differences were significant at less than the .001 level, with increasing age associated with poorer recall performances. The percent of recall variance accounted for by age was 17 and

18 percent for the second and third, respectively, as determined by ω^2 analyses. If it is recalled that the variance analyses by which the two ω^2 statistics were computed were underestimates of how difficult the second and third paired-associate tasks were for older people, it would be seen that the percentages of 17 and 18 are also underestimates. Table XXVII, together with the variance analyses, indicate substantial differences among age groups in paired-associate recall. Performances past age fifty were low, even among those who were tested and completed the procedures; subjects in their seventies could barely learn the list to the criterion within the ten trials.

As with the first paired-associate task, education group differences were significant ($p < .001$) only when they were ordered last in the step-down analyses. When the effects of education were adjusted for those of age and sex, differences between education groups were not observed ($p > .05$). Paired-associate learning and recall was seen, therefore, to be related more to the age of the subject than to the level of education.

Serial Learning

The ordered (structured) recall performances and the free recall performances were each analyzed in an analysis of variance which included scores of all subjects who completed the tasks. The results were similar to those of paired-associate performance, viz. statistically significant age differences even when excluding subjects who did not take or complete the procedures. After adjusting for education and sex effects, age differences were significant at less than the .001 level in the case of ordered recall and less than the .01 level with free recall. The ω^2 analyses indicated that 19 percent and 7 percent of the ordered and free recall performances, respectively, were accounted for by the age of the subject. As with the paired-associate data, these are regarded as underestimates of the effect of age on performance. Up to age fifty, serial recall performances differed little with age; after fifty, however, and especially in the seventies, poorer performances were seen.

Unlike the paired-associate data, serial learning and recall was related to education level even after adjusting for the effects of age and sex differences. This was so for the free recall performances ($p < .0001$) as well as the ordered recall performances ($p < .01$). Sex differences were not observed ($p > .05$).

While performance was better on free recall than on ordered recall ($p < .02$), as seen in a mixed design analysis of variance, it made little difference in regard to age which type of recall task was given. The interaction between age and type of recall task yielded an F-ratio of 0.87 ($p > .05$).

Delayed Recall

The six age groups were compared in regard to the number of items they recalled after a period of delay in relation to the number they recalled immediately after learning. For each subject, two recall scores were recorded: 1. the number recalled on the last trial given soon after the regular learning procedure, and 2. the number recalled after the delay. This was done with each of the three paired-associate tasks and the ordered recall of the serial learning tasks, using only the data of those subjects who were given and able to carry out the original procedures. A univariate analysis was carried out for each of these four tasks which may be seen in Table XXVIII.

The source of variation of central interest in each of these analyses is the interaction between age and immediate versus delayed recall. The question is: Relative to the level of initial recall or initial learning, is the delayed recall poor for the older subjects than for the younger? Table XXVIII shows that with the first, i.e. easy paired-associate task, the answer is no; the interaction between age and the two types of recall tasks was not significant, neither was the overall age effect ($p > .05$). With the second paired-associate task, the interaction between age and initial versus delayed recall was significant at less than the .01 level. Figure 10 demonstrates clearly that, with advanced age, delayed recall tended to be less good relative to initial recall. The tendency was similar with both the third paired-associate task and the serial learning task,[1] as can be seen in

---

[1] Four subjects did not complete or were not given the serial learning task. Their scores were estimated for both initial and delayed recalls from the respective cell means.

TABLE XXVIII

ANALYSES OF VARIANCES OF DELAYED (D) VERSUS INITIAL (I) RECALL ON FOUR ROTE LEARNING TASKS

Source	PA-1* df	F	PA-2* df	F	PA-3* df	F	SL-1* df	F
Between Subjects	119		99		83		119	
Educ. (E)	1	.02	1	20.43†	1	32.37†	1	22.51†
Sex (S)	1	1.37	1	2.02	1	.31	1	1.38
Age (A)	5	.72	5	5.47‡	5	6.77†	5	4.80†
A X S	5	.67	5	4.54‡	5	.50	5	1.49
Residual**	107	.08	87	2.26	71	4.55	107	2.23
Within Subjects	120		100		84		120	
D versus I (DI)	1	6.46‖	1	22.55†	1	3.84	1	126.75†
E X DI	1	.02	1	.06	1	1.75	1	19.53†
S X DI	1	1.37	1	.16	1	.41	1	1.09
A X DI	5	.72	5	3.47§	5	2.49£	5	2.56£
A X S X DI	5	.67	5	1.93	5	1.04	5	.78
Residual**	107	.08	87	.60	71	.75	107	1.75
Total	239		199		167		239	

* Test descriptions: PA-1 = easy paired-associates task, both stimulus and response associates were meaningful words; PA-2 = more difficult version of PA-1; PA-3 = difficult paired-associate task, stimuli were two-letter consonants and response associates were meaningful words; SL-1 = serial learning task of ordered recall.

** Residuals are reported as mean squares. All other sources of variation are represented by F-ratios.

† $p < .0001$; ‡ $p < .001$;
§ $p < .01$; ‖ $p < .02$;
£ $p < .04$;

Figure 10, but the tendencies were of marginal significance ($p < .04$).

Overall, then, the evidence for a decrement in delayed recall with age over and beyond decrement in initial recall was unequivocal in only one of four tests that were made. A tendency toward decrement in delayed recall was seen in two other tests as well, but it must be concluded that what problems aged people may have in delayed recall, they are probably secondary to those of initial recall. Each of the four F-ratios associated with the interactions between age and initial versus delayed recall was small even when statistically significant (see Table XXVIII). Moreover, as determined by the ω^2 analyses, the percent of performance variance (delayed recall versus immediate recall) which may be predicted by knowledge of the age of the subject was so small as to be inconsequential. For each of the two more

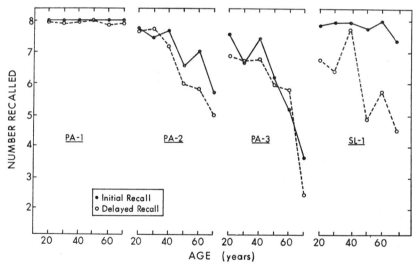

Figure 10. Initial and delayed recall as a function of age. Four tasks are represented: PA-1 = easy paired-associates task, both stimulus and response associates were meaningful words; PA-2 = more difficult version of PA-1; PA-3 = difficult paired-associates task, stimuli were two-letter consonants and response associates were meaningful words; SL-1 = serial learning task of ordered recall.

difficult paired-associate tasks and for the ordered recall of the serial learning tasks, ω^2 was only 1 or 2 percent.

CONCLUSIONS

Paired-associate learning and recall, serial learning and recall are less good for older adults than younger ones. This much seems evident based upon the procedures and results of this chapter. This, plus the data bearing on delayed recall and the results of Chapter 9 on long-term memory, suggests that memory difficulties in later life may be due less to memory storage and less to memory retrieval than to registration of information in the nervous system. There are a variety of published reports which are compatible with this emphasis on initial learning rather than on delayed recall (e.g. Jerome, 1959; Hulicka and Weiss, 1965; Davis and Obrist, 1966; Moenster, 1972).

There is little or no controversy that learning *performance* on paired-associate tasks and serial learning tasks tends to decline in later life. However, there is controversy as to the reason for this. There are those who maintain and have brought evidence to bear that much or all of the age decline is due, not to learning or registration, but to aspects of the testing procedure that affect the ability of older people to demonstrate what they have learned. Typically, the aspect of the procedure investigated is the speed of experimental pacing, i.e. the speed with which the items to be learned are presented. For example, Canestrari (1963), Arenberg (1965), and Monge and Hultsch (1971 demonstrated clearly that quick pacing of paired-associate tasks makes for poorer performances on the part of elderly subjects than slow or self-pacing. Similarly, Eisdorfer, Axelrod and Wilkie (1963) and Eisdorfer (1965) showed poor performance resulted from quick pacing of serial learning tasks. These investigators concluded that much of what seems to be a learning-recall deficit in later life turns out to simply be a performance problem. As the speed of experimental pacing increases, older people progressively show an inability to express what they have learned; they do not necessarily fail to learn what is required.

All this has a direct bearing on the data of the present study. Do the procedures and results reported here reflect an age-related difficulty in learning-recall rather than on performance factors? We think that they do.

First, all the studies in the literature, perhaps with the exception of that by Monge and Hultsch, show that even with the slowest of the experimental pacings, the older adults performed less well than the young. But more to the point of the present study, the three paired-associate procedures provided approximately five seconds for the response associate to be made to the stimulus of the pair. The literature suggests that, while this may not necessarily be the optimum time permitted for response by the elderly, it is long enough to be close to this time. The two serial learning tasks, in providing only a second between words in the list, may have put a burden on the performance mechanisms. Disregarding the serial learning data, therefore, the paired-associate data alone suggest a learning difficulty in later life. The difficulty is highlighted by yet another consideration.

The first, easy paired-associate task was presented to all subjects with the same experimental pacing as that used in the two more difficult paired-associate tasks. If pacing was the reason for the poor performances on the part of the elderly with the two difficult tasks, poor performance should have been manifest also with the easy task. This was not so, the performances of the elderly with the easy task were as good as those of the young, and this was good indeed. All age groups learned the task within only a few trials and were able to demonstrate this without problem; the experimental pacing of the testing procedure posed no difficulty for the older subjects. Not being able to perform well with the difficult tasks could not, therefore, be a reflection of pacing. It is more likely that it is a reflection of their not having learned the information.

All told, then, paired-associate learning and perhaps serial learning as well were seen to decline with age. This was taken as an index of registration in recall.

CHAPTER TWELVE

NEW LEARNING AND RECALL OF MEANINGFUL AND SILLY INFORMATION

IT WAS CONCLUDED in the previous chapter that the ability to recall new learning seems impaired in later life. This conclusion, however, was based on a type of new learning which is largely artificial and at least partly meaningless outside the laboratory. Rote learning, of lists of simple words and of word pairs that are related only arbitrarily, is not the kind of information people seek. While ability in rote learning of word lists may be helpful in everyday life, as, for example, items to be purchased in a store or in learning symbols in chemistry classes, activities such as these have personal relevance well beyond those seen in paired-associate learning and serial learning as practiced in the laboratory.

The present chapter is concerned with determining whether the recall of new learning is also difficult for the aging when the information to be learned is meaningful, involving the sequential redundancies of everyday spoken English. The present chapter examines this by presenting spoken paragraphs of English language which contain a variety of information and then testing for the recall of it. Age groups were not only compared for information of this type when the paragraph conveyed logical facts, but also when it conveyed illogical or silly ones.

PROCEDURES

Two main procedures were used, the first in two parts and the second in four parts. The former was of the logical information, the latter of the silly information.

First, each male and female subject was instructed: "I am going to read you a short story three or four sentences long. Listen very carefully. When I finish I will ask you to tell me exactly what I read."

> Thousands of persons / have been evacuated / from their homes / in two / Mexican states / after more than forty-eight hours / of rains / that have caused / disastrous floods. / Several lowland sections / in three cities / were reported under water. / One flooding river / has covered / almost a half million acres. / No casualties were reported./

The slash marks in the paragraph above denote separate items of information. Each one recalled was scored as 1.

A second paragraph was read as soon as the subject recalled all that he could of the first one.

> A short circuit / in machinery / that cools the penguins / forced keepers / to become icemen / Sunday / at the City zoo. / The temperature / in the penguin house / rose / from 50 degrees / to 75 / which is scorching / for the penguins. / A truck / was dispatched / and returned / quickly / with three tons / of ice. / None / of the birds / showed ill effects / from the brief / heat wave./

Again each memory was scored as 1. The total score for each subject was the sum of scores of both paragraphs.

Later in the test battery four separate silly information sentences were read, each followed by a test of recall. The four sentences were:

> 1. The Declaration of Independence / sang / overnight / while / the cereal / jumped / by the river./
> 2. Two days / ate / the bed / under the car / seeing / pink flowers / forever./
> 3. They slept / in the fire / to avoid the draft. / It was cold there / and their sweaters kept them / cool./
> 4. I eat pink mice. / They are delicious / but their green fur / gives me heartburn./

The recall score for each subject with these silly information sentences was the sum of scores of the four sentences.

RESULTS

Recall of the meaningful and of the silly information was analyzed separately since the latter involved less information per reading than the former. A decision was made beforehand, in the absence of other data, that paragraphs of silly information of the same length as the meaningful might be too difficult to use.

TABLE XXIX

ANALYSES OF VARIANCES OF LOGICAL AND
ILLOGICAL INFORMATION TEST SCORES

Source	df	Logical Information F	Silly Information F
Educ. (E)	1	8.29§	25.99†
Sex (S)	1	16.16‡	8.84§
Age (A)	5	4.93‡	8.12†
A X S	5	1.11	1.34
Residual*	107	34.74	9.60
Total	119		

* Residuals are represented by mean squares. All other sources of variation are represented by F-ratios.
† $p < .0001$
‡ $p < .001$
§ $p < .01$

Table XXIX is of two variance analyses, one for the meaningful and one for the silly information; both yielded similar results. Age, sex, and education groups were significantly different, with confidence levels ranging from less than .01 to less than .001 (see Table XXIX). When education group differences were adjusted for age and sex effects, significance was no longer achieved in the case of meaningful information ($p > .05$), although it was in the case of silly information ($p < .01$).

The nature of these significant results is indicated by Table XXX (estimated means) and by Figure 11 (observed means). Increased age was associated with poorer recall performances both of the logical and illogical types. As determined by ω^2 analysis, the percent of recall variance that could be accounted for by age was 12 with meaningful information and 19 with the

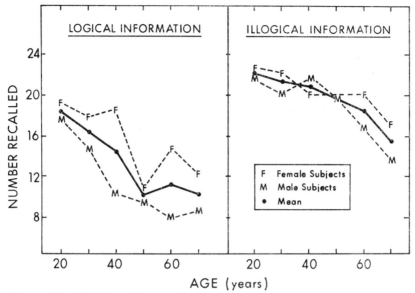

Figure 11. Number of items of information recalled as a function of age and sex. The information, in sentences of syntactically correct spoken English, was of two types: logical and illogical information. The two types are not comparable in terms of level recalled. Only age and sex comparisons within each type are meaningful.

silly. It would seem from this that age is associated more with poor recall of silly information than meaningful.

Women performed better than men but this sex difference was unrelated to age; the interactions between age and sex were not significant with either type of recall ($p > .05$). Those with twelve or more years of schooling recalled more information than those with less than twelve years of formal education.

CONCLUSIONS

A simple question was the basis for this brief chapter: Does the ability to recall new learning of meaningful information

TABLE XXX

RECALL OF MEANINGFUL AND SILLY INFORMATION:
ESTIMATED PERFORMANCE MEANS BY AGE DECADES

Tasks	20s	30s	Age (Years) 40s	50s	60s	70s
Meaningful Information	18.2	16.0	14.3	10.2	11.6	10.4
Silly Information	21.9	20.7	20.6	20.0	19.0	15.6

decline with age? The meaningful information was oriented around sequential redundancies of logical spoken English. A secondary question involved decline of ability with age in the recall of meaningful English in the sense of correct syntax, but not of logical information. The results of this study showed decline with both types of information, logical and illogical.

The age-associated decline was moderate in terms of correlation between recall performances and age, with the magnitude of correlation being the greater for the recall of illogical information than logical. Table XXX indicated a somewhat greater mean difference among age groups in meaningful information than silly information, but in terms of an age-recall association, the extent was greater with the silly. The difference in correlations could be due to differences in the difficulty of or in the meaningfulness of the information, i.e. in the personal relevance of it.

At face value, learning the illogical information is the harder and as such may account for the greater age effect. However, the illogical information was presented in small units and thus was made easier. The amount of illogical or silly information retained relative to the amount possible was greater than that of logical information, i.e. the percent retained was larger. Accordingly, task difficulty would not appear to be an adequate answer for the stronger relationship between age and recall with the silly information.

Chapter 9 might provide a clue. It was seen in that chapter that the personal relevance of information may minimize age differences in the ability to recall. In the present chapter, the more relevant information, the meaningful rather than the silly, may have similarly minimized age differences, making for lower correlation between age and recall.

Even if this interpretation is correct for the present data, it does not follow necessarily that the concept of relevance or meaningfulness applies in this way in every context. Subsequent chapters, particularly the next one, will disclose a different pattern. Different procedures and different levels of difficulty of information provide other roles for the concept.

CHAPTER THIRTEEN

RECALL OF NONVERBAL VISUAL INFORMATION

CHAPTERS 11 AND 12 indicate that the ability to recall what was very recently experienced is less good for older adults than for younger ones. Moreover, there is a suggestion in these chapters that the difficulty older people have in recall may be exacerbated if the experience is not relevant or meaningful to them and if the recall is based upon rote memory processes.

Chapters 11 and 12 involve verbal information auditorily presented. Would the same apply with information which is nonverbal and visual in character? The present chapter is an attempt to answer this question, utilizing both recognizable (relatively meaningful) visual forms and unrecognizable (meaningless) ones.

PROCEDURES

Recall and Placement of Recognizable Forms

Nine cards, each with a recognizable form printed on it, were placed on a table in front of the subject. The nine cards, each 2¾ inches square, were put in random places on the table, but each card was positioned upright, not inverted or rotated.

Along with the random placement of the nine cards, a large card containing all nine forms was presented. Figure 12 is the large card reduced in size; the actual size was of the nine 2¾ squares.

The subject was instructed, "I am going to show you nine cards. Each card has a different design on it. You will also see a large card. The large card has nine squares on it. In each square is a design. These designs match the ones on the nine small

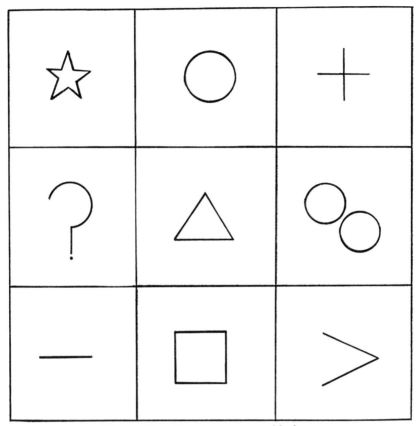

Figure 12. The nine recognizable forms.

cards. When I tell you to begin I want you to place each of the small cards in one of the squares on the big form. Put the small card in the square which has the same design in it as the one on the card."

Thus far the task was a simple matching task. Following this, all the task materials were removed and a blank card was presented. The blank card was identical to the large one depicted as Figure 12, except that the designs or forms were not there. The subject was instructed: "Now I want you to try to remember what each shape was and which square it belongs in. Draw each shape in the right square."

Two scores were given to each subject: 1. A score of 1 was

given each correct recall (drawing) irrespective of their place-ment on the blank page. Thus, 9 was the maximum score possible. 2. An additional score of 1 was given if the recall was placed correctly. The maximum score here, therefore, was 18.

Reproduction of Meaningless Shapes

This procedure involved the recall of four shapes, each designed to represent nothing that is recognizable or meaningful. The four shapes may be seen as Figure 13.

Each subject was presented with the first shape and instructed, "Now I am going to show you some . . . figures . . . I want you to study them carefully. When I take the card away I will ask you to draw the figure you just saw, as best you can, on one of these blank sheets of paper."

Each shape was presented individually in the order indicated in Figure 13. The shape was exposed for five seconds and the drawing-recall of it was without time limit.

The shapes in Figure 13 were made up of straight lines forming a number of connections or points. The four shapes had twelve, five, eleven, and five points, respectively. The recall performances of the subjects were scored on the basis of the points that the subjects drew, both extruding and intruding. The absolute difference in the number of points the subject drew in recalling the shape, and the actual number of points of the shape determined the score. For example, if a subject drew a shape of eleven points in recalling the first, twelve-pointed shape, and another subject drew a shape of thirteen points, both subjects would receive a score of 1. The four shapes were scored in this way, and the sum of the four scores represented the subject's recall performance. This score was subtracted from twenty to reverse the direction so that high scores represent good performances.

RESULTS

Each subject was represented by three scores, two for the procedure of recognizable forms and one for the procedure of meaningless shapes. A multivariate analysis of variance was not

Figure 13.   The four meaningless shapes.

carried out with the two procedures because three female subjects of the oldest age and higher education group were not given the latter procedure. The reason for their not being tested was unrelated to their abiilty or to other aspects of their roles as subjects. Thus, only analyses of variances were carried out, two for the form placement procedure and one for the procedure of meaningless shapes.

Recognizable Forms

CORRECT RECALL. Subjects were scored for the correctness of their recalls regardless of whether or not they placed the forms in the correct areas of the large card (of nine squares).

TABLE XXXI

ANALYSES OF VARIANCES OF NON-VERBAL
VISUAL INFORMATON TEST SCORES

Source	df	Recognizable Forms Recall F	Recognizable Forms Recall & Placement F	Meaningless Shapes Recall df	Meaningless Shapes Recall F
Educ. (E)	1	8.62†	5.90‡	1	0.42
Sex (S)	1	0.41	0.41	1	1.72
Age (A)	5	3.90†	3.44†	5	1.98
A X S	5	0.81	0.58	5	1.44
Residual*	107	3.09	11.33	104	9.53
Total	119			116	

* Residuals are represented by mean squares. All other sources of variation are represented by F-ratios.
† $p < .01$
‡ $p < .02$

It may be seen in Table XXXI that although the six age groups were significantly different ($p < .01$) in regard to recall performances, the age-recall relationship, as seen in Table XXXII and Figure 14, was not systematic. In the main, however, decline in correct recall was more typical of the old than of the young, the association, as determined by ω^2 analysis, was 10 percent.

Table XXXI also shows significant education group differences ($p < .01$). Those with more than twelve years of formal schooling tended to perform better than those with twelve or less years. When, however, education group differences were adjusted for age and sex effects, significance was no longer found ($p > .05$).

The two sex groups were not different in recall, nor was the interaction between age and sex significant ($p > .05$).

CORRECT RECALL AND PLACEMENT. Here, the subject was scored for both the correctness of recall and correct placement (on the card of nine squares). It was more difficult to make a

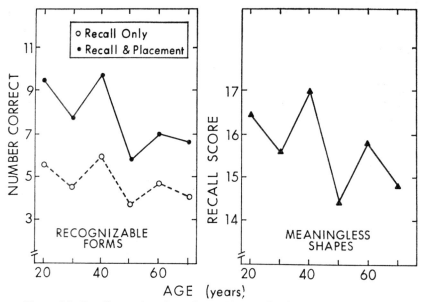

Figure 14. Recall as a function of age. The recalls of 9 recognizable forms were each scored as "1" if correct (O). Each was given an additional score of "1" if placed correctly on a large card (●). The recall of meaningless shapes (▲) was scored on the basis of the number of connections or points that were recalled (drawn). See text.

TABLE XXXII

RECALL OF NONVERBAL VISUAL INFORMATION:
ESTIMATED PERFORMANCE MEANS BY AGE DECADES

Tasks	Age (Years)					
	20s	30s	40s	50s	60s	70s
Recognizable						
Recall only	5.31	4.08	5.66	3.75	4.98	4.14
Recall & Placement	9.18	7.07	9.43	5.85	7.32	6.81
Meaningless Shapes	16.51	15.70	17.06	14.39	15.73	14.82

Note: Nine recognizable forms were recalled and scored as number correct. A score of 1 was given for each correct recall plus a score of 1 for each correct placement. Meaningless shapes were scored on the basis of the recalled number of connections or points that were drawn. (See text. The higher the number, the better the recall performance.)

top score than when only correct recall was considered because it required memory of two aspects of the information. In this sense, it was a more stringent task.

The results with this scoring were similar to that of recall only. Table XXXI shows that the six age groups and the two education groups were significantly different, and in the same way as with recall only. This is not surprising since the two scores are related, the less stringent one involving the recall only score. Again, the education difference was not seen when adjustments were made for age and sex effects. The ω^2 for age was .09, similar to the 10 percent of recall variance accounted for by age when only recall and not placement was credited.

Meaningless Shapes

Table XXXI shows that for neither age, sex, nor education groups were differences found statistically significant ($p > .05$). Table XXXII and Figure 14 suggest age trends similar to that of the recall of recognizable forms. These trends were not significant, however, regardless of whether or not adjustments were made for education and sex effects.

CONCLUSIONS

This chapter was begun with a statement of results found in Chapters 11 and 12, viz. the recall of recent experience was less good for older people than younger, at least as it applied to the verbal information that was presented auditorily. The data of this chapter dealt with nonverbal visual information. There were two procedures: one of these, recognizable forms, also reflected an age difference in recall; the other, meaningless shapes, did not. All these data together, then, suggest that both types of experience, verbal-auditory and nonverbal-visual, may be seen more difficult to recall for older people than younger.

This chapter was also begun with a suggestion that meaningful information may more readily be recalled by the elderly than the young, relative to the recall of meaningless information. The present data did not bear this out but two items of experimental method must be emphasized to better understand this.

The two procedures, recognizable forms and meaningless shapes, are not comparable; they may not be compared in terms of the correctness of recall or of age differences in the correctness of recall. The recognizable forms procedure was more akin to a latent learning task than to a learning task where there is clear intent to learn and remember the information. The subjects were given a matching task without instructions to learn the forms, and then, afterward, without warning, they were tested for recall. Here, the older subjects performed more poorly than the young. The meaningless shapes procedure, on the other hand, had clear instructions to learn and memorize. Age groups were not different. Perhaps it was this difference in procedure, the nature of the scoring, the difficulty of the task, or the one five-second exposure rather than several exposures; whatever the reasons, age differences were not found.

Taken together, then, the data of Chapters 11 and 12, in suggesting that personally relevant information will be relatively well retained by aged people, and the data of the present chapter, in indicating that the meaningless shapes were no more difficult for the old than for the young, suggest that the concept, meaningfulness, by itself, is not sufficient without regard to procedural factors and the others indicated. Despite this, as already indicated, it can be concluded from the results of the present chapter and those of Chapters 11 and 12 that both the recall of verbal-auditory and nonverbal-visual information seem to be less good in later adult life than during earlier adulthood.

CHAPTER FOURTEEN

RECOGNITION MEMORY

T HE MEMORY STUDIES discussed to now have been of recall (Chapters 9-13), the search and retrieval of information from a memory store. The present chapter focuses on recognition memory as distinguished from recall memory. Recognition is measured by the identification of information that has been learned or experienced, rather than the retrieval of it. It is thought that both recall and recognition require search of information in the memory store, but instead of retrieval, recognition is characterized by a matching of information that is in the store with information in the environment (e.g. Schonfield and Robertson, 1966). For this reason, it is thought, measures of recognition reflect that more is in the memory store than can be recalled.

This model distinguishing between recall and recognition, although limited, has utility in explaining the relative difficulty in recall as compared to recognition. It serves to highlight areas of difficulty aged people may have in remembering events and experiences. While the major area of difficulty in recall is thought to be retrieval, Fozard and Waugh (1969) provided data suggesting that storage may also be a problem. Recognition memory, on the other hand, i.e. the matching of information in the memory store with that in the environment, is often thought to be of no special difficulty for the aged (e.g. Schonfield and Robertson, 1966; Kapnick, 1971). As will be seen, this may not be so.

PROCEDURES

Four tasks constituted the recognition memory battery; two tasks were of verbal materials and two were of nonverbal. The former were of words presented visually and auditorily. The latter were of meaningful objects and of meaningless shapes, both presented visually.

Word Stimuli

VISUAL. The subject was instructed, "I am going to show you a list of words. Study the list carefully. When I take it away I am going to ask you to pick out these words from a much longer list of words."

With these instructions the subject was given a card showing a list of eight words typed in bulletin size. The list was presented for ten seconds, followed by a longer list of thirty-two words. The subject was then told, "Now circle the words you saw." After eight words were circled, the thirty-two-word display was removed.[1]

letters in length. The thirty-two-word display, presented in two lists of sixteen words each, was composed of eight words of each letter length (two through six). The thirty-two-word display may be seen in Appendix C.

The procedure was then repeated with a comparable list of eight stimulus words and a comparable thirty-two-word display. The second list of eight words in their order were: wheat, budge, day, end, north, maid, shape, loss. Both the words in this list and in the first one and those in both thirty-two-word displays were arranged randomly in terms of their letter-lengths.

The score for each subject was the number of correct recognitions (circled words) in both lists. Thus, the top possible score was 16.

AUDITORY. The procedure was similar to that of the visual presentation except for one important difference. Instead of the eight stimulus words being presented at once, they were presented one at a time. The subject was instructed, "We are going to do the same thing again. This time, however, I will read the words to you." The eight words in order were: bed, part, front, wealth, lip, wall, speech, knife. The thirty-two-word display was presented in the same way as in the visual presentation.

The auditory procedure was repeated with the following word

---

[1]The eight stimulus words were in the following order in a list: school, net, range, fish, yard, branch, map, noise. It will be noticed that two words were three letters in length, two were four letters, two were five, and two were six

list: porch, milk, sound, lot, task, job, figure, worker. Again, the thirty-two-word display was presented visually.

The top score possible was 16, one point for each correct recognition.

Nonverbal Stimuli

OBJECT RECOGNITION. The subject was instructed, "I am going to show you a card with pictures of four objects on it. Study the pictures carefully. When I take the card away I am going to ask you to pick out these four objects from a much larger group of objects."

The four stimulus objects were the house, fish, coat, and basket among the sixteen-object display seen as Figure 15. The four objects were given to the subject for study for five seconds. When the card was removed the subject was given the sixteen-object card to circle the four objects. As with the word stimuli, no time limit was imposed in circling recognized items. The top possible score was 4.

SHAPE RECOGNITION. This procedure involved meaningless shapes similar, but not identical, to those seen in Figure 13 of the previous chapter. The present recognition procedure was different from the other recognition procedures in that only one stimulus was presented prior to recognition testing. This was so because it was thought beforehand that the presentation of several stimulus shapes at once would make for a recognition task that was too difficult to do.

Figure 16 is of sixteen shapes, four of which were the stimulus shapes, and the remainder, the distractor ones. Each subject was instructed: "I am going to show you some cards. On each card is a drawing of a figure. Study it carefully. After I take the card away I am going to ask you to pick out the figure from a larger group of figures like it."

First a card with a single drawing was presented (the fifteenth one in Figure 16, counting from left to right and top to bottom). This form was presented for five seconds and then withdrawn. Figure 16 was then presented and the subject was asked to point to the "figure you just saw." This was repeated with a second

Figure 15. The 16 objects shown to the subjects. Among these are 4 which they had seen previously.

stimulus shape (the fifth in Figure 16), then a third stimulus (third figure in Figure 16), and, last, a fourth stimulus (the twelfth figure).

The score for each subject was the number of correct recognitions. Thus, top possible score was 4.

Figure 16.   The 16 shapes shown to the subjects.   Among these are 4
which they had seen previously.

RESULTS

The recognition performance scores of the four procedures
were included in a multivariate analysis of variance (with the
step-down, least-squares solution described in Chapter 2, section
on Data Analysis and Presentation).   Age effects were ordered

last in the analysis and differences were statistically significant ($p < .02$). The two education groups were also different ($p < .0001$), but the two sex groups were not ($p > .05$). Neither was the interaction between age and sex significant ($p > .05$). The statistically significant results of this multivariate analysis permitted univariate analysis of each of the four procedures.

Visual Word Recognition

Table XXXIII shows that word recognition performance was significantly different among the six age groups ($p < .01$), even after making statistical adjustments for the effects of education and sex differences. Table XXXIV and Figure 17 show that the

TABLE XXXIII

ANALYSES OF VARIANCES OF FOUR RECOGNITION TASK SCORES

Source	df	Tests			
		Visual Word	*Auditory Word*	*Object Recognition*	*Shape Recognition*
Education (E)	1	10.29‡	2.94	0.06	21.19†
Sex (S)	1	2.94	1.15	0.71	0.97
Age (A)	5	4.15‡	0.12	1.54	2.17
A X S	5	1.01	0.87	0.46	0.59
Residual*	107	6.46	5.15	0.05	0.38
Total	119				

* Residuals are represented by mean squares. All other sources of variation are represented by F-ratios.
† $p < .0001$
‡ $p < .01$

nature of the difference was of poorer recognition performances with increasing age. Eleven percent of the recognition performance variance was accounted for by the age of the subject, as determined by ω^2 analysis. When age was ordered first in the analysis (not shown here), i.e. when adjustments were not made for education and sex effects, the relationship between age and performance (ω^2) was increased to 18 percent.

Those subjects with more than twelve years of formal education performed better than those with twelve or less years ($p < .01$). However, this only held when education was not adjusted for age and sex. When so adjusted, education group differences

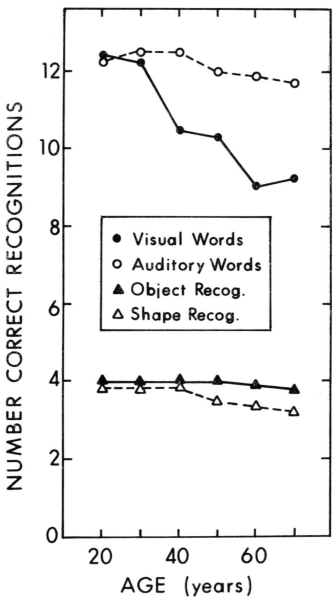

Figure 17.   Mean recognition scores as a function of age. The top scores possible on the word tasks were "16"; the top scores on the others were "4."

were not significant ($p > .05$). No other sources of variation were significant in Table XXXIII.

Auditory Word Recognition

Unlike the preceding visual procedure, no sources of variation were statistically significant with the auditory presentation of stimulus words ($p > .05$). This was true whether the ordering of variables was as seen in Table XXXIII, or whether age was ordered first and education last. The visual and auditory procedures, as indicated, were different in the way the stimulus words were presented; the visual presented all eight words at once, and the auditory presented the eight words one at a time. Whether it was this difference in procedure or the sensory modality that made for the differences in results is not possible to determine from the present study. What does seem clear from the data of Table XXXIV and Figure 17 is that the younger

TABLE XXXIV

RECOGNITION MEMORY: ESTIMATED PERFORMANCE
MEANS BY AGE DECADES

Tests*	Age (Years)					
	20s	30s	40s	50s	60s	70s
Visual Word	12.39	12.22	10.54	10.35	9.07	9.31
Auditory Word	12.30	12.42	12.45	12.01	11.96	11.73
Object Recognition	4.02	4.03	4.02	4.00	3.93	3.84
Shape Recognition	3.88	3.77	3.78	3.52	3.49	3.24

* The score for each test was the number of items correctly recognized. The top scores possible were 16 in the word tests and 4 in the others. Scores higher than 4 in the latter tests are due to statistical estimates resulting from adjustments for education and sex differences.

subjects performed about as well, i.e. recognized about as many words, in one procedure as the others, but the older subjects performed better in the auditory situation. This was borne out statistically in a single mixed design analysis of variance (not shown here) in which responses to both procedures were examined. The interaction between age group and type of procedure (visual versus auditory) was significant ($p < .01$).

Object Recognition

No source of variation was statistically significant with respect to object recognition. This was so whether education was ordered first and age ordered last in the step-down analysis (as seen in Table XXXIII) or whether the reverse ordering was made in the analysis.

No source of variation was statistically significant ($p > .05$) probably because the task turned out to be such a very simple one. Table XXXIV and Figure 17 show that top or near top scores were made by all age groups. In addition, the performance variances were very small. (Table XXXIII shows that with a residual mean square of 0.05, no F-ratio was larger than 1.54.)

Shape Recognition

As with object recognition, high scores were achieved by all age groups in shape recognition. Although this task was more difficult than the object recognition task, it also turned out to be too easy from the perspective of performance variation. Table XXXIII shows that only education groups were significantly different ($p < .0001$). When age was not adjusted for education and sex differences, significance was seen here too ($p < .001$). Figure 17 shows a slight decline in performance with age; as determed by ω^2 analysis, Figure 17 depicts a 14 percent association between age and shape recognition variance.

CONCLUSIONS

Four procedures were used to test recognition memory. Only with one of these (visual word recognition) was there an unqualified age effect: 11 percent of the performance variance was accounted for by the age of the subject. In one other procedure (shape recognition) there was an age effect only when adjustments were not made for education and sex differences. This latter analysis, as indicated earlier in the book, is the one typically made in studies on aging.

In all four procedures trends of age decline were seen and were reflected in a significant overall age difference in the multivariate analysis of variance. Taken together, then, the data of this chapter suggest that recognition memory, like recall memory, declines with age, although the decline may not be manifest with tasks that are easy.

Schonfield (1965) and Schonfield and Robertson (1966) presented a list of twenty-four words, one at a time, and then tested for recognition memory by placing each word with four others. Age differences were not observed. Similarly, Kapnick (1971) failed to find an age effect with stimulus word lists as long as forty. Despite this long list length, Kapnick's tasks were relatively simple since each stimulus word was shown with only one other for the subject to indicate recognition memory. Perhaps the difficulty of the task is the key to whether recognition difficulties in later life will be demonstrated.

A study by Schonfield, Trueman and Kline (1972) on recognition memory in dichotic listening and a study by Erber (1974), just completed at this writing, are the only two we know that show a clear age effect in recognition memory, other than that reported here. In addition, there is the study by Fozard and Waugh (1969) that demonstrated poorer recognition memory with age for those items in a list that were recalled less well. Of these studies showing age deficits, Erber's is the most typical of recognition studies. She had two stimulus word lists: one, like that of Schonfield (1965), was twenty-four words in length, and the other was more difficult, sixty words in length. Recognition testing was accomplished by embedding each stimulus word along with four others. Erber reported that subjects of mean age seventy years recognized fewer words than younger adults of mean age twenty-three years, but task difficulty (list length) had no differential effect with respect to age. Thus, task difficulty does not seem the key concept, unless made more specific as follows.

Neither Erber nor Schonfield et al., nor we in this chapter would claim that recognition memory declines with age to an extent as large as that of recall memory; in fact, the claim would be just opposite. But, each of these studies indicated recognition memory deficits with age, contrary to the earlier studies. Two aspects of recognition memory are important to consider. If the task is difficult in the sense that many words need to be learned, i.e. registered and stored, then poor performance may reflect difficulty in this process rather than in the searching and matching of the information in the memory store with that in the environmental displays. When, however, the registration task is easy but the search and matching process is not, poor recognition performance may reflect the latter process. The visual word data in the present study, and possibly the shape recognition data as well, suggest this: eight and four items to be learned are not difficult tasks, but searching for them in a display of thirty-two and sixteen items, respectively, provides much opportunity for error.

CHAPTER FIFTEEN

CONCENTRATION AND INTERFERENCE

T HE PREVIOUS SIX CHAPTERS dealt with different types of memory/learning in relation to age. Age-decline was found with several types, but not all. Those which demanded much concentration and attention, at least at the time the information was first acquired, seemed especially difficult for the aged. Thus, concentration and attention may be a key in understanding memory in relation to age.

Another key may be a favorite explanatory concept of psychologists studying memory/learning: interference. Forgetting is often explained on the basis of competition from other events or experiences.

The present chapter is of concentration and interference in recall. The role of task difficulty in relation to these two factors was also investigated. Are older subjects especially poor in recall when the task requires much concentration, involves interference, and is difficult?

PROCEDURES

Two procedures were used: the first was of Following Instructions and the second was of Digit Span. Following Instructions was in two subparts and Digit Span in four subparts.

Following Instructions

NONINTERFERING. Each subject was given a stack of papers, each paper having on it a square, a triangle, and a circle, in this order going from left to right. (Each side of the square was 2 inches, each leg of the triangle was 2¼ inches, as was the diameter of the circle. Each sheet of paper on which the three figures were presented was approximately 8½ inches wide and 3¾ inches high.)

The subject was instructed, "I'm going to read you some directions. The directions will tell you to put a number in one of the forms. . . . For example, if the directions I read say, 'Put a 2 in the triangle,' you put a 2 in the triangle. Now you try one. The directions are, 'Put a 1 in the circle and a 2 in the square.'"

Five graded levels of difficulty in task instruction were given, each level composed of two tasks; thus ten instructions were given in all. The easiest level had one element to recall and carry out, the most difficult level had five elements. For example, the first of the two easiest instructions (level one) was: "Put a 1 in the circle." The first of the most difficult level (level five) was: "Put a 3 in the square, a 2 in the circle, a 1 in the triangle, a 2 in the square, and a 1 in the triangle." It is seen by the above that task difficulty is synonomous with memory load; each succeeding level had one additional element to recall. The ten instructions may be seen in Appendix C.

Each subject was given five scores, one for each of the five levels of task difficulty. The scores were of percent errors. For example, performances on the two tasks of level one could result in two errors (100 percent), one error (50 percent), or no errors (zero percent). Performances on the two tasks of level five could result in ten errors (100 percent), no errors (zero percent), and in percentages in between, in steps of 10 percents. The other levels were scored similarly; this enabled age comparisons in interaction with task difficulty levels.

INTERFERING. There were again five difficulty levels of the instruction tasks, but instead of placing numbers in the geometric forms, the same types of geometric forms were placed. Thus, the first difficulty level instruction was, "Make a small square in the triangle." The first task of difficulty level five was, "Make a circle in the square, a square in the circle, a triangle in the square, a square in the triangle, and a triangle in the circle." The total sequence of this intratask interference battery may also be seen in Appendix C.

Digit Span

WITHOUT DISTRACTION. Chapter 10 described several procedures, among these were Digit Span forward and Digit Span backward. That chapter may be referred to for the specific details of these digit span procedures since the associated data are examined in the present chapter again. This time, however, they are examined in comparison with similar data collected under conditions of interference or distraction.

In the digits forward procedure of Chapter 10, the subject recalls orally the digits which had been presented to him. The digits backward procedure requires a recall of the digits in opposite order. Thus, if the subject hears seven, two, four, he would respond four, two, seven.

The digits were presented in a graded series of increasing length, the longest being eight and the shortest being three (in some instances two). There were two presentations of each digit length, with the procedure terminated when incorrect recalls were made in response to both presentations.

WITH DISTRACTION. The Digit Span procedure of the present chapter was also given in a forward and backward manner. The subject was instructed, "I am going to read you some more numbers. Again when I finish I want you to say the numbers after me. But this time I want you to do something in addition to remembering the numbers I say. I want you to tap your knuckles on the desk the whole time we are doing this." A demonstration of tapping was at the rate of two per second.

The two types of digit tasks (with and without distraction) permitted examination of the relative difficulty older subjects may have with interfering distraction.

RESULTS

Following Instructions

The variance analysis had these five main effect variables: education, sex, age, conditions of interference (i.e. numbers versus geometric forms), and levels of task difficulty (i.e. number of elements in the instruction). The four sources of variation in

Memory, Related Functions and Age

TABLE XXXV

ANALYSES OF VARIANCES OF SCORES ON TWO TASKS INVOLVING
INTERFERENCE AND VARIABLE DIFFICULTY

| | *Tasks* | | | |
| | *Following Instructions* | | *Digit Span* | |
Source	*df*	*F*	*df*	*F*
Between Subjects	119		119	
Education (E)	1	19.06†	1	13.11‡
Sex (S)	1	0.04	1	1.36
Age (A)	5	8.26†	5	5.97†
A X S	5	1.03	5	1.29
Error I*	107	388.80	107	3.04
Within Subjects	1080		360	
Interference (I)	1	3.41	1	0.72
E X I	1	0.49	1	0.17
S X I	1	0.85	1	2.13
A X I	5	1.96	5	2.23
A X S X I	5	0.37	5	3.71§
Error II*	107	222.36	107	0.74
Difficulty (D)	4	193.64†	1	219.57†
E X D	4	2.79‖	1	1.49
S X D	4	1.05	1	1.09
A X D	20	2.15§	5	1.17
A X S X D	20	0.82	5	0.44
Error III*	428	218.15	107	1.37
I X D	4	23.57†	1	3.63
E X I X D	4	2.14	1	6.15£
S X I X D	4	0.57	1	1.50
A X I X D	20	1.12	5	0.98
A X S X I X D	20	0.89	5	2.24
Error IV*	428	135.96	107	0.59
Total	1199		479	

† $= p < .0001$; ‡ $= p < .001$;
§ $= p < .01$; £ $= p < .02$;
‖ $= p < .05$

Note: In the Following Instructions task, the source of variation, *Interference*, refers to the comparison of placing numbers in the geometric forms versus placing other geometric forms in the forms. In the Digit Span task, *Interference* refers to the comparison of the tapping procedure versus that of not tapping.

The source of variation, *Difficulty*, refers to the 5 levels or number of elements placed in the geometric forms in the instructions task and to whether the recall was forward or backward in the span task.

* Error terms are represented by mean squares, other sources of variation by F-ratios.

Table XXXV of major interest for present purposes are: age (A), the interaction between age and conditions of interference (A X I), the interaction between age and task difficulty (A X D), and the second order interaction of age, interference, and difficulty (A X I X D).

Table XXXV shows that, of these sources of variation of major interest, only age ($p < .0001$) and the interaction between age and task difficulty ($p < .01$) were statistically significant. Figure 18 (observed means) and Table XXXVI (estimated means) show clearly that increased age was associated with poorer performance. (Unlike the variance analysis of Table XXXV, where percent errors were the data analyzed, Table XXXVI and Figure 18 are in terms of percent correct—the higher the score, the better the performance.)

Figure 18 and Table XXXVI also show that it wasn't until three elements had to be remembered that performance was impaired appreciably in any age group. The significant interaction between age and task difficulty was such that those of increased age were seen as performing less well as the task became more difficult.

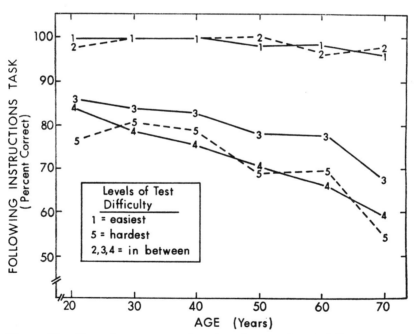

Figure 18. Percent correct as a function of age and task difficulty. Combined scores of two tasks: placing numbers in geometric forms and placing other geometric forms in the forms.

TABLE XXXVI

CONCENTRATION AND INTERFERENCE: ESTIMATED
PERFORMANCE MEANS BY AGE DECADES

Tasks	Age (Years)					
	20s	*30s*	*40s*	*50s*	*60s*	*70s*
Following Instructions*						
No Interference						
Level 1	99.50	99.10	99.50	100.10	98.10	97.80
Level 2	97.36	99.74	99.86	100.03	93.92	96.34
Level 3	91.36	87.61	85.52	82.40	81.04	74.69
Level 4	83.89	84.88	80.77	80.85	68.83	63.16
Level 5	70.13	75.03	71.13	70.27	65.15	59.32
Interference						
Level 1	99.71	99.49	99.71	97.56	100.34	95.17
Level 2	99.93	99.87	99.93	100.01	100.09	97.54
Level 3	80.26	79.80	81.10	74.28	74.02	60.34
Level 4	85.75	73.23	70.75	61.10	64.10	56.43
Level 5	81.51	82.03	85.51	68.50	75.98	69.99
Digit Span**						
Forward	7.26	7.27	7.11	6.71	6.85	6.18
Backward	5.67	5.98	5.62	5.49	4.36	4.16

---

* The Following Instructions tasks were scored in terms of percent correct. Scores higher than 100 percent are due to statistical estimates resulting from adjustments for education and sex differences.

** The Digit Span tasks were scored in terms of the number of digits recalled. The data in this table refer to the procedure in which the subject kept tapping his knuckles on the desk while recalling the digits. Data of the span procedure without such tapping may be seen in Table XXV, with tests listed as ADF and ADB.

All the foregoing notwithstanding, neither the statistically significant age effect nor the significant interaction between age and task difficulty was seen as important in terms of the percent of performance variance that could be predicted by these sources of variation. As determined by ω^2 analysis, only 3 percent of the performance variance could be accounted for by the age of the subject, and only one percent could be accounted for by knowledge of both age and level of task difficulty.

Table XXXV shows other significant sources of variation. Very clearly, the more difficult the task, the poorer the performances that resulted, irrespective of the age of the subject ($p <$ .0001). And, although the performance scores were not significantly different for the two conditions of intratask interference, they were significantly different when task difficulty was involved: the interaction between task interference and task difficulty (I X D) was significant at less than the .0001 level. However, this interaction was not systematic and amenable to interpretation.

Two other sources of variation in Table XXXV were statistically significant. Those of higher education performed better than those with less education ($p < .0001$), and tended to do so as the difficulty of the task increased (E X D, $p < .05$). However, both these sources of variation involving education were no longer seen as significant ($p > .05$) when education was ordered last in the step-down analysis (not shown here).

Digit Span

There were also five main effect sources of variation in Table XXXV of the Digit Span data: education, sex, age, interference or distraction (tapping versus no tapping) and difficulty or type of task (digits forward versus digits backward). Again, there were four sources of major interest: age (A), the interaction between age and interference (A X I), between age and type of task (A X D), and between age, interference, and type of task (A X I X D).

Of these four sources of variation, Table XXXV indicates that only age differences were statistically significant ($p < .0001$); the indicated interactions were not statistically significant ($p > .05$). Although the recall performances tended to decrease with increasing age (see Figure 19 and Table XXXVI), in terms of explained variance (ω^2), the age of the subject accounted for only 7 percent of the variance.

Backward recall was poorer than forward recall ($p < .0001$), but unanticipated was the finding that the distraction of the tapping procedure did not affect overall performance. The difference between digit span recall without interfering tapping and with it was not statistically significant ($p > .05$). These results may be seen most clearly, perhaps, in Figure 19. Only prominent in this figure is the age effect and the fact that recall is easier when it is forward than backward.

Table XXXV indicates a significant interaction between age, sex, and whether or not the recall task involved tapping (A X S

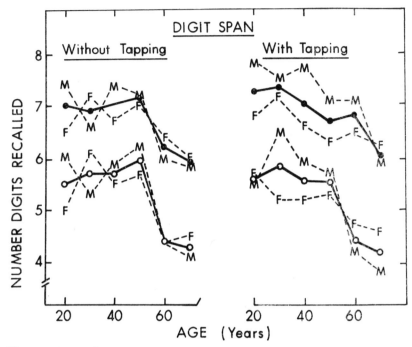

Figure 19. Auditory digit span as a function of age and sex. Closed circles represent Digit Span forward and open circles represent Digit Span backward. M = male subjects; F = female subjects. Tapping was by the subjects while performing the recall tasks.

X I, $p < .01$); Figure 19 shows this complex function. It may be seen that it is so complex that it is not easily interpreted and summarized. The small F-ratio (3.71) associated with this inter-action, together with the very small percent of recall variance it accounts for (1 percent), suggests that much attention to it is not indicated.

Those subjects with more than twelve years of education were seen to perform better than those with twelve or less years, but only when education was ordered first in the step-down analysis ($p < .001$). When ordered last, education groups were not significantly different ($p > .05$). One interaction involving education level was significant whether or not education was ordered first—that of education, condition of tapping, and whether the task was forward or backward (E X I X D, $p < .02$). In general, the less educated groups performed relatively poorly when the task was backward recall and with the distraction of tapping.

CONCLUSIONS

The Following Instructions task, designed as a measure of concentration, reflected less good performances on the part of the elderly than the young. Two aspects of these results must be emphasized. First, what was here called concentration may be none other than another type of memory. Following Instructions requires memory of what needs to be done; it is possible that the concentration required is not different from that in other memory tasks. Second, whether the age decrement is concentration, memory, or some combination of the two, only 3 percent of the performance variance was accounted for by the age of the subject.

Susceptibility to interference, over and beyond concentration, was ascertained by the comparison between that part of the task which involved placing numbers in geometric forms and that part which involved placing geometric forms in larger, similar ones. Interference, as measured this way, was not a problem for any age group, not young or old.

Similar to the Following Instructions procedure, the intended interference in the Digit Span task was no special problem for the subjects. Interference in the Following Instructions task was thought to derive from the competing similarity of the task stimuli. The interference in the Digit Span task was thought to derive from the competing attention and activity of the tapping. There are many sources and varieties of interference; thus, while those of the present study presented no special problem in relation to the age of the subject, other types may.

CHAPTER SIXTEEN

MEMORY/LEARNING: SUMMARY AND PRINCIPAL COMPONENT ANALYSIS

T HE INTRODUCTORY REMARKS in Chapter 8 on age-related behavior apply here in regard to memory/learning. While advanced age was associated with relatively poor memory performances, as was low education level, and the two sexes were not very different in how they performed, there were important exceptions. For example, the studies in long-term memory (Chapter 9), which will shortly be summarized along with the other types of memory, indicated that the age groups were not different overall, but the two sexes were different, women performing much the worse.

The confounding effects of age and education present in the data of Chapters 3 through 7 (Part I) were present also in the memory/learning data of Chapters 9 through 15 (Part II). Thus, the statistical analyses testing for age differences in memory performance were designed to minimize the confounding influence of education levels. This was done by the use of hierarchical, step-down solutions. It was pointed out that such analyses are conservative in terms of the probability values associated with the statistical tests of the observed age differences. These values may be seen in Table XXXVII. More traditional tests of age differences undoubtedly would have yielded more highly significant results.

The estimates of the relationships between the performance variances and the ages of the subjects were computed by the statistic, ω^2. Table XXXVII shows that, in terms of the percent of performance variance accounted for by age, the range of ω^2 was between near zero and at least 20. Since the ω^2 statistic is

TABLE XXXVII

SUMMARY OF AGE DIFFERENCES IN MEMORY

(Chapters 9 through 15)

Procedures	Chapter	Age Differences (p)	ω^2
Long-Term Memory	9		
Period: 1950-1969**		Not sig.	
1930-1949**		< .03	.06
1910-1929**		Not sig.	
1890-1909**		Not sig.	
Spans	10		
Auditory Digits Forward		< .01	.10
Auditory Digits Backward		< .001	.13
Auditory Letters Forward		< .001	.12
Auditory Letters Backward		< .02	.07
Visual Digits Forward		< .01*	.09*
Visual Digits Backward		< .02	.07
Patterns	10		
Auditory		< .01	.12
Visual		Not sig.	
Kinesthetic		< .01*	.10*
Short-Term Memory	11		
Paired Associates 1		Not sig.	
Paired Associates 2		< .001	.17+
Paired Associates 3		< .001	.18+
Serial Learning 1		< .001	.19
Serial Learning 2		< .01	.07
Delayed Memory	11		
(PA 1)—(Delay)		Not sig.	
(PA 2)—(Delay)		< .01	< .02
(PA 3)—(Delay)		< .04	< .02
(SL-1)—(Delay)		< .04	< .02
Paragraphs	12		
Logical		< .001	.12
Silly		< .0001	.19
Visual Forms	13		
Recognizable 1		< .01	.10
Recognizable 2		< .01	.09
Meaningless		Not sig.	
Recognition	14		
Auditory Words		< .01	.11
Visual Words		Not sig.	
Meaningful Objects		Not sig.	
Meaningless Objects		< .001*	.14*
Concentration	15		
Following Instructions 1**		< .01	.11
Following Instructions 2**		< .0001	.20
Digit Span: Tapping vs. No Tapping		Not sig.	

————

* Statistically significant age effect only when age ordered first in the stepdown analysis. ω^2 based on age ordered first.

** Not reported in text in this form.

based upon the conservative hierarchical, step-down solution, it is, itself, a conservative estimate of age-performance relationships. Again, more traditional analyses would have indicated greater relationships. For example, the ω^2 of .20 in Table XXXVII became .26 when the analysis was carried out as it more typically is.

SUMMARY (CHAPTERS 9 THROUGH 15)

There were seven categories of memory/learning. The first, long-term memory performance (Chapter 9), as indicated, did not decline with age. However, there were different age patterns for the recall of memories associated with different historical time periods. For example, as Figure 8 demonstrates, for events occurring during the era 1910-1929, little or no age-memory performance relationship pattern was seen. On the other hand, for the period 1930-1949, performance improved to about age fifty and then declined. The data of these long-term memory studies suggested that it is the impact value or importance to the subject of the experience that determines how long a memory can be recalled. Important memories can be life-long.

Memory for spans and patterns was investigated next (Chapter 10). This type of function, it was said, might be thought of in one of two ways. It could be thought of as a type of very short-term memory where little or no time for rehearsal or practice is possible; thus, perhaps, little or no long-term retention might be expected. It could also be thought of as a memory which is even more fleeting, as a "passing through" of information, perhaps by-passing the process of memory registration and true storage. Conceived in this way, it is not unlike the perceptual system (P system) of Broadbent (1958) or the primary memory (PM) of Waugh and Norman (1965). As will be seen later, the first interpretation is probably the more sound, but, in any case, the age-recall relationship was such that the age of the subject accounted for approximately 10 percent of the performance variance. The published literature indicates, however, that the actual correlation between age and performance is contingent upon a variety of procedural factors, most notably the number of items to be recalled and the speed with which the items are presented. The greater the number and speed, the greater the difficulty the aged have in the recall.

Chapter 11 was concerned with two aspects of memory. It discussed a type of short-term memory which more obviously involved registration than the memory investigated in Chapter 10, and it also discussed delayed recall. Age was a large factor in recall as measured by the paired-associate and serial learning performances. As the procedures were administered here, many of the aged subjects would not or could not perform the task at all.

Delayed recall of this learning also was age-related, although the relationship was small relative to the registration-recall measurements. As may be seen in Table XXXVII, only about 2 percent of delayed recall variance was accounted for by the age of the subject. This statistic, however, may be spurious. Delayed recall was measured for only those subjects able or willing to carry out the paired-associate and serial learning procedures. Perhaps, if it were possible to measure delayed recall for those subjects whom we were not able to test, especially those extraordinarily poor in the immediate recall, the difficulty with age in delayed recall might have been more manifest.

Paired-associate and serial learning tasks are not very typical of everyday life situations. Accordingly, more common memory/learning tasks were given in Chapter 12. Short paragraphs of meaningful content were read to the subjects with tests of recall made soon afterward. In addition, to determine whether meaningful content is an important factor, sentences of silly or illogical information were also read, with recall tests following. Table XXXVII shows that both types of memory performance declined with age, the former age-performance relationship accounting for 12 percent of the variance, the latter, 19 percent. It was suggested that, like the data of long-term memory of Chapter 9 and under certain circumstances, personally meaningful information minimizes whatever age deficit there may be in recall.

All the memory/learning tasks discussed thus far were verbal in nature; in Chapter 13 two nonverbal memory/learning tasks were presented. One of the tasks involved recognizable visual forms, such as circles and triangles, and the other task involved meaningless, nonsense forms. The former task was scored in two different ways, represented as Recognizable 1 and 2 under Visual Forms of Table XXXVII. A statistically significant general age decline in the recall of these visual forms was seen only with the recognizable forms, not the meaningless. Age accounted for approximately 10 percent of the performance variance with the former task.

Comparison between the two tasks of Chapter 13 was not possible because of the way in which the tasks were given. The recognizable forms task, but not the meaningless forms task, was more akin to one of the latent learning than to one of traditional recall. Thus, it may be the latent learning more than recall of nonverbal recognizable forms that made for the age effect.

All the memory/learning tasks above were of recall performance. Recognition performance was measured in Chapter 14. There were four measurements of recognition, two involving words and two involving objects. Reliable age patterns were seen in only one of the four procedures (recognition of words presented auditorily, $\omega^2 = .11$), but recognition of meaningless objects also showed a trend toward age decline. The older literature indicating little or no age effect in recognition memory was challenged by these data when viewed in conjunction with more recent published reports.

An effort was made to investigate concentration and interference in Chapter 15. Two tasks of following instructions were given, each requiring very close attention to the specific instructional details; the subject recalled one part of the instructions while subsequent parts were given. The second of these tasks was thought to require even more concentration than the first because there were interfering aspects of the specific details.

Two digit span tasks were also given, one forward and one backward. As a source of interference or distraction designed to test concentration, the subject was required to tap his knuckles on the desk while performing the span tests. These performances were then compared to those in which tapping was not required.

The Following Instructions tasks reflected an age pattern, as did the Digit Span tasks, but interference effects were no greater for older people than for younger. The age of the subject accounted for 11 and 20 percent of the performance variances on the two Following Instructions tasks, respectively, while age accounted for 7 percent of the span performance variance.

All told, therefore, many types of memory/learning performances, but not all, were seen as age-related. Moreover, among those that were age-related, not all were to the same extent. The organization of these memory performances is presented next.

PRINCIPAL COMPONENT ANALYSIS

The guideline suggested by Cattell (1952) in regard to the minimum ratio of number of measurements to subjects, followed in Chapter 8, was followed here too, with very minor deviation. Cattell suggested that a minimum of four subjects be tested for each measurement used in a principal component analysis. The 120 men and women subjects tested here permit thirty measurements, according to the guideline.

Table XXXVII indicates thirty-four measurements; the last one listed, including both forward and backward spans, made for thirty-five measurements in all. These thirty-five plus three more—one for age, sex, and education—made for thirty-eight scores, eight of them too many for Cattell's guideline. The following variables were eliminated from analysis: the two tapping procedures of Chapter 15 (the last listed in Table XXXVII) were eliminated because they did not make for the intended distraction. The correct recall score of the recognizable visual forms procedure of Chapter 13 was kept, but the alternate score involving placement was eliminated. The second and third paired-associate tasks data were eliminated since many data were missing due to the many subjects who failed to complete the tasks. The corresponding delayed recall data were also eliminated.

This left twenty-eight scores plus three for age, sex, and

education, a total of 31 variables—one more than the Cattell guideline suggests. This extra measurement was judged a negligible deviation from guideline for principal component analysis, and the thirty-one variables, listed in Table XXXIX, were kept.

There were three types of measurements in the principal component analysis which were different from that reported in the text. The delayed recall measurements of Chapter 11 were computed in terms of difference scores, i.e. differences between the immediate recall score and the delayed recall score (each in terms of number correct). This difference score was then subtracted from 8 (the poorest score possible) to reverse directions. The difference score made for a degree of independence between the delayed recall and the memory/learning scores. The Following Instructions task of Chapter 15 was reported originally in terms of five levels of difficulty. For the purpose of principal component analysis, these levels were collapsed and overall correct recalls were scored.

Correlations

The thirty-one variables were intercorrelated, as may be seen in Table XXXVIII. Coefficients of correlation in this table are significant at the 5 percent level if approximately 0.17 or higher, and significant at the one percent level if approximately 0.23 or higher. Of the 465 correlation coefficients, 200 were 0.23 or higher.

Components

The data of Table XXXVIII were subjected to a principal component analysis, with the results seen in Table XXXIX. Four factors were rotated, this number being based on an asymptote criterion of the percentage of explained variance associated with each of the unrotated factors (Cattell, 1966; see footnote 1, Chapter 8). The first four factors accounted for 48 percent of the variance.

The first factor accounted for 16 percent of the performance variance after rotation; age was very prominent on this factor (a loading of −.67), with education level less so (.47). Advanced age and lower education were associated with poor performances. This factor appears to be a general one in that several, but not all, types of memory are represented. Notably missing or present only to minor extent were long-term memory and memory for spans and sequential patterns. The three test variables contributing most to this factor were the two serial learning tasks (loading .74 and .71, respectively) and the logical paragraphs tasks (.72). The silly paragraph task was also represented on this factor (.56), as were other functions—the second Following Instructions task (.53), Visual Word Recognition (.55), and Recognition of Meaningless Objects (.55).

There were four procedures which loaded less highly on the first factor: Paired Associates (.47); Delayed Recall of Serial Learning (.40); plus two which were represented more highly on the third factor, Kinesthetic Patterns and Auditory Letter Span Backward. These latter two were represented with loading only in the .30s.

Although this memory factor is not an all-inclusive one, it is a general type of short-term memory factor which is neither uniquely verbal nor nonverbal; neither uniquely of visual nor of auditory stimuli; neither uniquely of meaningful nor of nonsense material; and not confined to recall as compared to recognition memory. As indicated, this type of general factor was an age-related one—as age increased, memory/learning performances decreased.

The second factor is easiest to label and interpret. It is a long-term memory factor, accounting for 11 percent of the variance after rotation, with the four long-term memory tasks loading highly on it (.85 to .66). Only the sex of the subject was represented here other than the four tasks: the representation was a loading of −.60, with women having performed much poorer on these tasks than the men. Since there is no reason to think that mechanisms of memory are different for men than women, it may simply be that it is the scope or type of information that is different between the sexes.

In constructing the long-term memory tasks for the purposes of age comparisons, the assumption was made that the required

MATRIX OF CORRELATION

	1	2	3	4	5	6	7	8	9	10	11	12	13
1. Age		02	—48	—22	—09	01	—02	—31	—33	—36	—40	—34	—29
2. Sex			03	—25	—40	—41	—46	—05	—04	—01	—15	—04	—11
3. Education				35	29	21	16	17	32	27	31	32	14
4. Long-Term Memory 1					59	28	19	11	16	12	28	19	18
5. Long-Term Memory 2						69	65	17	21	08	23	16	24
6. Long-Term Memory 3							62	14	15	—02	13	18	11
7. Long-Term Memory 4								18	11	03	17	19	11
8. Auditory Digits Forward									47	50	53	39	43
9. Auditory Digits Backward										52	62	37	37
10. Auditory Letters Forward											49	25	39
11. Auditory Letters Backward												24	40
12. Visual Digits Forward													26
13. Visual Digits Backward													
14. Patterns, Auditory													
15. Patterns, Visual													
16. Patterns, Kinesthetic													
17. Paired Associates 1													
18. Serial Learning 1													
19. Serial Learning 2													
20. (PA 1)—(Delay)													
21. (SL 1)—(Delay)													
22. Logical Paragraphs													
23. Silly Paragraphs													
24. Visual Forms, Recognizable													
25. Visual Forms, Meaningless													
26. Auditory Words													
27. Visual Words													
28. Meaningful Objects													
29. Meaningless Objects													
30. Following Instructions 1													
31. Following Instructions 2													

————————

Note: For all tests high scores represent good performances and low scores represent poor

XXXVIII

COEFFICIENTS (r), $N = 120$

14	15	16	17	18	19	20	21	22	23	24	25	26	27	28	29	30	31
—41	—21	—34	—15	—50	—51	—02	—36	—42	—53	—23	—10	—13	—44	—19	—38	—43	—48
—09	03	—14	—02	—09	—04	11	—12	30	18	—07	—28	09	12	08	05	—02	—06
24	12	24	15	39	38	10	30	24	40	19	—02	10	22	02	29	31	21
—01	14	10	07	28	30	12	16	20	18	13	09	14	14	—03	20	11	12
03	03	01	10	27	15	05	19	11	06	23	13	09	11	00	10	06	04
02	—03	—02	07	09	09	10	17	12	03	17	05	09	—02	—14	05	—06	—01
03	—08	03	05	14	12	02	13	01	—00	14	15	05	05	—05	08	00	05
36	40	21	10	14	26	07	11	—02	41	19	02	24	22	25	13	26	25
41	37	35	23	27	38	16	20	18	58	22	04	10	22	11	30	37	24
38	34	31	09	28	37	07	13	17	51	08	13	07	21	23	17	45	29
47	38	43	26	41	45	13	27	27	53	25	23	16	37	22	34	40	30
34	24	29	06	22	30	25	43	02	30	22	—06	20	22	02	22	23	19
37	22	23	19	23	38	08	22	18	33	25	14	08	26	15	14	26	35
	30	59	11	25	30	02	23	37	27	22	29	07	29	15	26	27	27
		23	01	03	05	04	16	02	23	06	04	15	13	08	07	26	19
		11	24	34	07	23	20	30	16	23	06	29	01	25	29	28
			33	31	17	05	29	28	07	10	07	30	04	23	15	26
				54	02	37	40	47	19	13	22	41	24	30	38	40
					22	35	36	54	22	16	08	34	25	47	47	39
					03	02	15	—02	—12	—01	09	—04	16	10	12
						24	21	25	26	25	28	—01	26	23	26
							47	19	—01	06	44	20	30	23	28
								27	—04	19	39	28	28	34	27
									04	04	01	14	16	11	30
										—08	02	04	03	08	07
											42	08	—01	02	07
												21	24	27	19
													03	34	21
														28	31
															46

performances. All coefficients multiplied by 100.

TABLE XXXIX

ROTATED FACTORS OF PRINCIPAL COMPONENT
ANALYSIS OF DATA IN TABLE XXXVIII

Variable	*Factors*			
	1	*2*	*3*	*4*
Subject Description				
1. Age	—.67	—.02	—.34	—.06
2. Sex	.13	—.60	—.14	.49
3. Education	.47	.27	.18	.25
Long-Term Memory				
4. Period: 1950-1969	.25	.66	.05	.15
5. 1930-1949	.12	.85	.05	.04
6. 1910-1929	.00	.84	—.01	.10
7. 1890-1909	.02	.82	.04	—.06
Spans				
8. Auditory Digits Forward	.00	.13	.75	.22
9. Auditory Digits Backward	.24	.13	.68	.18
10. Auditory Letters Forward	.23	—.04	.69	.03
11. Auditory Letters Backward	.39	.18	.66	—.01
12. Visual Digits Forward	.14	.24	.47	.39
13. Visual Digits Backward	.25	.16	.53	—.04
Patterns				
14. Auditory	.27	—.02	.66	—.19
15. Visual	—.08	—.05	.64	.18
16. Kinesthetic	.32	.00	.50	—.21
Short-Term Memory				
17. Paired Associates 1	.47	.06	.02	.00
18. Serial Learning 1	.74	.18	.12	.01
19. Serial Learning 2	.71	.13	.28	.00
Delayed Memory				
20. (PA 1)—(Delay)	.09	.06	.08	.37
21. (SL 1)—(Delay)	.40	.24	.19	.18
Paragraphs				
22. Logical	.72	—.03	—.08	.15
23. Silly	.56	—.05	.46	.30
Visual Forms				
24. Recognizable 1	.26	.22	.21	—.03
25. Meaningless	.12	.16	.20	—.66
Recognition				
26. Auditory Words	.10	.10	.14	.49
27. Visual Words	.55	—.02	.18	.29
28. Meaningful Objects	.29	—.19	.22	—.06
29 Meaningless Objects	.55	.07	.13	.05
Concentration				
30. Following Instructions 1	.48	—.07	.42	—.07
31 Following Instructions 2	.53	.00	.30	—.12
Percent Variance	16	11	15	6

information was *at one time* equally represented (in memory storage) among the six age groups: thus, what differences among them were manifest may be attributable to memory function, probably retrieval. Even if this assumption is valid for the age groups, it may not be so for the sex groups. Women may simply not have acquired, in the first place, as much of the information as did the men. Women performed more poorly than men, but the age groups were similar in their overall performances.

The third factor accounting for 15 percent of the variance after rotation was a memory for spans and patterns factor. All the tasks of Chapter 10 were represented—their loadings ranged from .47 (Visual Digit Span Forward) to .75 (Auditory Digit Span Forward). Age was represented in a more minor way than in the first factor; as age increased, performance of spans and patterns decreased. The loading of age, however, was only —.34.

This factor was not a pure span and pattern factor since three other tasks were also represented. There were the first and second Following Instructions Tasks (.42 and .30, respectively) and the memory for the Silly Paragraphs task (.46). But these loadings are small and, in the main, it was the Span and Pattern tests which dominated this third factor. The fact that both spans and patterns were highly represented suggested that these are similar, at least related functions; perhaps the distinction between spans and patterns is not indicated.

Both the forward and the backward span recalls loaded highly on this factor. This might suggest that the passing-through conceptualization of span recall discussed in Chapter 10 is less adequate than one pointing to the similarity between this type of recall and other short-term memory types. Backward recall suggests some holding of the information in a memory store, otherwise it would be necessary, as it was in Chapter 10, to conceptualize the passing through as a read-out in reverse. However, if span recall is more akin to short-term memory than to passing through, it does not seem to be identical to it, as judged by the different task loadings on the first and third factors. Spans data are not rehearsed or practiced as much as typical short-term memory data, as, for example, the serial learning of words. Perhaps the organization scheme discussed by Kay (1968) in Chapter 10 is relevant here: Span recall (third factor) may lie somewhere between the primary stimulus trace (a peripheral sensory function) and a longer term trace associated with more apparent registration and storage (first factor). It is suggested that the span and pattern recall is not as transient as primary memory (PM) of Waugh and Norman (1965), but not as durable as their concept of secondary memory (SM).

The fourth rotated factor accounted for only 6 percent of the variance and, in the main, appeared to be associated with the recall of Meaningless Visual Forms (−.66). Four other test variables were found on this factor: two were with loadings in the .30s and two in the .40s. This factor is a poor one in the sense that only one loading was very high, and no meaningful psychological interpretation could be imparted. This factor suggested that, as ability to recall or reproduce meaningless forms increased, there was a tendency to be less able in other memory functions: Delayed Paired Associates (.37), Auditory Word Recognition (.49), Silly Paragraph recall (.30), and Visual Digit Spans Forward (.39). This pattern was somewhat more true of men than women (the loading of sex was .49). Again, too much attention to this fourth fatcor does not seem indicated.

CONCLUSIONS

In generalized summary, then, three of the four rotated factors were psychologically interpretable. The first was age-related and encompassed a large variety of short-term memory functions; highly educated people performed relatively well on tests of these functions. The second factor was sex-related and basically it was a long-term memory factor. The third factor was of spans and sequential patterns; increased age was related to relatively poor performance here, but to an extent less than with the functions of the first factor.

This describes what was found in the factor rotation, but left undescribed what was not but could have been found. The tests used in this study were designed to reflect individual differences with respect to sensory mode, meaningful vs. nonsense material, verbal vs. nonverbal stimuli, differences in holding functions such as spans forward vs. backward, and recognition vs. recall memory. None of these were differentiated; only the differences between span, short-term memory, and long-term memory were differentiated. Thus, advanced age was seen to negatively affect short-term and span recall, but no particular aspect within these categories more than another. Long-term memory was not a function of age except that, as seen in Chapter 9, different information long in storage may result in different age patterns.

The major variables in terms of their loadings and the factors that were extracted were: Factor 1 (General Short-Term)—Age, education, serial learning, and memory for paragraphs; to a somewhat lesser extent, visual word recognition, meaningless object recognition, and Following Instructions were also found; Factor 2 (Long-term memory)—Sex and only the long-term memory tasks were represented with high loadings; Factor 3 (Spans and Patterns)—all the span and pattern tasks were highly represented. Other tasks were represented to a lesser extent. These were the tasks of Following Instructions and silly paragraph recall. Age was represented here, but to an extent less than on the first factor.

CHAPTER SEVENTEEN

MEMORY/LEARNING AND RELATED BEHAVIOR: SUMMARY DISCUSSION AND PRINCIPAL COMPONENT ANALYSIS

I~N~ C~HAPTER~ 1, at the very beginning, it was indicated that many abilities and functions were investigated here as they related to adult age. Memory function was the prime focus and constituted more than half of the data that were collected. It was pointed out that it is very difficult, if not impossible, to distinguish between memory and learning operationally; thus the function was called here memory/learning.

In addition to the investigation of memory/learning (Part II of this book), there were five other foci of investigation (Part I). These were brain function involving perceptual abilities, psychomotor speed, intelligence, personality and morale, and health and health habits. Each of these five functions was analyzed separately in detail and described in individual chapters.

The data of these latter foci of investigation were integrated and summarized in Chapter 8; the memory/learning data, constituting seven chapters, were integrated and summarized in Chapter 16. In the present chapter, both sets of data, i.e. those of Part I and those of Part II, were integrated.

Chapter 2 described the subjects of this study. They were 120 adult men and women, ten men and ten women in each age decade from the twenties through the seventies. The women were given all the procedures, but the men were not. They were given all the memory/learning tasks and about half of the other ones.

It is a well-documented fact that any random sampling of adults within the general population will result in a group of people showing progressively less formal education with increasing age. This was true of the present sample also. To minimize the effects of educational factors in the analysis of age differences in performance, a special type of statistics was used. It was pointed out in several places in this book that these statistics did not eliminate the educational or cultural influences, they only minimized them; in so doing, maturational factors were thought to be maximized. Thus, the statistical tests used here with respect to age were considered conservative ones, suggesting confidence in the positive results which were found.

SUMMARY DISCUSSION

Memory/Learning

Again in Chapter 1, it was said that there is disagreement as to whether short-term memory and long-term memory are subserved by different mechanisms. It was also said that the ability to recall information may be based upon different mechanisms than the ability to recognize what had previously been learned; recall and recognition memory may be different in their respective processes. To the extent that principal component analyses are relevant to these issues, the results of the present investigation clarifies them.

Chapter 16 described three psychologically meaningful factors. One was a general short-term memory factor, another was a long-term memory factor, and the third was one of span and pattern recall. This latter factor described a type of memory which may well be of even shorter-term duration than that often referred to as short-term memory.[1] If each of these three factors represents truly orthogonal (independent) functions, it could be concluded that not only are short- and long-term memory subserved by different mechanisms, but that there may be a third mechanism, one subsuming span and pattern recall. Both short-term memory functions were age-related, the general short-term factor being the more so. On the other hand, long-

---

[1]It may be akin to what Waugh and Norman (1965) called primary memory (PM), although it is conceived of here as being less fleeting. Waugh and Norman conceptualized PM as part of the short-term memory system.

term recall was not age-related; overall performances on the part of the elderly subjects with the long-term memory tasks were as good as those on the part of the younger adult subjects.

While the principal component analysis suggested the possibility of more than one mechanism of memory based on duration in storage, it provided no evidence that recall and recognition memory are different in regard to mechanism. This is compatible with the position of Tulving and Thomson (1971), for example, who indicated that both recall and recognition memory may involve retrieval and, therefore, are not intrinsically distinct processes.

In the present study, there were four tasks which were designed to measure recognition memory. Performances on two of them were represented on the general short-term memory factor along with measures of recall, and performance on one of them was represented on an uninterpretable fourth factor. Thus, the superiority of recognition memory over recall memory, and the relative difficulty elderly people have in the former, might be credited to the possibility that recognition tasks tend to be easier for reasons unrelated to mechanism. (For a discussion of task difficulty in recognition memory, see Botwinick, 1973, p. 277-279).

The memory/learning studies carried out here suggested that the primary difficulty that aged people tend to have is at the point of registration of information—at the point of acquiring it. Once registered, memory ability may not be nearly so susceptible to impairment processes as is usually thought. The bases for this conclusion are two findings. First, the three memory factors may be graded in terms of the degree of registration, of learning, required at the time of the experiment. The tasks of the general short-term factor required most registration and those of the long-term factor required none. All registration of information had been accomplished long prior to the time of testing in the present investigation. The spans and patterns factor required some registration at the time of testing but, as discussed in Chapter 16, successful performances may not have required it completely.

Age decrements in recall were seen in direct proportion to the extent of this grading in registration. There was no overall age decrement in the long-term memory task performances, some in the spans and patterns, and so much difficulty in the short-term tasks that many of the elderly subjects could not or would not do some of the tasks at all.

The second basis for believing that the registration phase of the memory processes is the crucial one in regard to age are the present data of long-term memory (Chapter 9). It will be recalled that people were asked to recall information of events that took place in various historical time periods. Older people were better in recall than young people of the events occurring in some periods and worse in recall of events of other periods. An examination of these events disclosed that recall was best for all age groups when the historic event took place when the subjects were aged between fifteen and twenty-five years.

It was suggested that it is impact value, or the importance of the information, that largely determines how well and how long it will be retained. Impact value or importance of the information bears on the concept of registration. It is thought that the more important the information is to the subject, that is, the greater impact the information has, the more likely it will be registered. Certain events, having made more impact on the elderly than on the young, result in recall scores superior to those of the young. An alternate notion is that impact is more a matter of peak biopsychological reactivity than of the personal importance of the information. In either case, however, impact and registration do not seem distinguishable operationally.

The studies in memory/learning attempted to discover whether, and how, the sensory modality by which information was acquired affected memory ability, especially among the aged. The studies also attempted to discover whether meaningful information relative to meaningless was better recalled by the elderly than the young. Verbal information is relatively well retained thoughout the lifetime, the present study sought to determine the relative roles of verbal and nonverbal information in the recall processes of older people. None of these considerations—not sensory mode, meaningfulness of information, nor verbal aspects of it—were differentiated in the principal component analysis. None of these seemed to play a role greater in one age group than another.

A most consistent result was the great extent of individual differences in the memory performances. With the possible exceptions of the relatively difficult paired-associate learning procedures, none of the task performances were predictable with great accuracy by the age of the subject alone. Many variables, procedural and others, determine performance scores.

Other Age-Related Functions

Two principal component analyses were carried out with the data categorized by the five groupings: 1. Brain function, 2. Psychomotor speed, 3. Intelligence, 4. Personality and morale, and 5. Health and health habits. There were two analyses because, as indicated, while women subjects were tested with all of the more than twenty procedures measuring these categories, men subjects were tested with approximately half this number.

When the concept, brain function, was introduced in Chapter 1, it was said that the procedures used to assess this type of function are often called tests of brain damage and tend to be perceptual in nature. Since there was no reason to think of the subjects in this study as brain-damaged and since such labeling is both speculative and potentially damaging, the term brain function/perception was used as preferable. The concept brain function/perception implies no pathology; instead, it implies a continuum of individual differences in function, much as do most all biological and behavioral processes. Yet, the idea that those on the lowest end of the continuum function behaviorally in a manner not unlike those with minimal brain damage must be entertained as a possibility.

The principal component analyses of Chapter 8, particularly the one based on both men and women subjects together, disclosed a most interesting result. Those subjects performing poorly on the brain function/perception tasks also performed poorly on the psychomotor speed tasks, i.e. they were slow in their responses. It was mostly aged subjects who performed in this way. These results are interesting in light of the conclusions of Hicks and Birren (1970, p. 377) who reviewed the research literature on "psychomotor slowing in aged and brain-damaged subjects":

> Behavioral, neuroanatomical, and neurophysiological evidence indicate that the basal ganglia with their complex neural connections are importantly involved in the speed of initiating and executing movements. Damage or dysfunction of the basal ganglia may be the basis for the psychomotor slowness.

It will be seen later, however, that the analysis of the present chapter replicates this relationship between brain function/ perception and psychomotor speed functions only partially. The nature of the partial replication, together with other data, suggested that a differentiation among types of brain function/ perception performance and among types of speed performances may be necessary. Such differentiation was made and will be discussed subsequently.

The analyses of Chapter 8 also showed that verbal intelligence is independent of the psychomotor slowing and the relatively poor brain function/perception performances that are associated with age. Neither age, speed, nor brain function/ perception was represented in a sizable way on the verbal intelligence factor. This finding is not unlike the conclusion of Reed and Reitan (1963, p. 273), discussed in Chapter 1: stored information based on prior experience (such as is inferred from verbal intelligence test scores) does not suffer with brain damage. On the other hand, problem solving ability of the kind which bears only little or not at all on past experience suffers much. There were not many tasks in the present study measuring such problem solving, but the one that was used (Block Design) loaded in the principal component analysis on the brain function/ perception factor. This formulation of independence between verbal intelligence and perceptual integrative ability is now classic (e.g. Botwinick, 1967); but, as will be seen, its generality is challenged by some of the data in the present chapter.

The measures of health and health habits reflected only little, if any, difference among the age groups. This minimal difference might be attributed to the efforts in sampling and recruiting subjects who could be given the many tests used in this study. The differences in health status with age that were found, as might be expected, were lower for the older subjects than for the younger ones. With one of the measures (Cornell, given to women only) low health scores tended to be associated with low scores of brain function/perception; this was not the case, however, with self-ratings of health.

Only minimal differences in personality with age were found. This seems to be in keeping with the general report that "personality type was independent of age" (Neugarten et al., 1964, p. 187). These minimal differences, however, were interesting in regard to what was seen in the principal component analysis. Those women whose test results pointed to a calculating pattern in their approaches to life—to a lack of forthrightness and naturalness in their interactions—and those women who seemed to be especially persevering and conscientious were the ones who tended to perform poorly on the brain function/perception and psychomotor speed tasks. It was speculated that the calculating and persevering behavior pattern may be helpful in defending against perceived failing ability.

PRINCIPAL COMPONENT ANALYSIS

Cattell (1952) suggested that in factor analysis the number of subjects should exceed the number of variables at least by a ratio of 4 to 1. This guideline was followed in Chapters 8 and 16 and was followed in the present chapter as well. Thus, there were thirty variables in the analysis of the data of men and women.[2] With the three subject variables of age, education, and sex, an additional twenty-seven task variables were allowed.

---

[2] An analysis was attempted also on the data of women alone. However, the restriction of fifteen variables, including the two of age and education, proved too severe for the analysis to be of much use. Some factors were not psychologically meaningful and this, it was thought, resulted from too few tests of a particular kind that could be brought under examination. Those factors that were psychologically meaningful were not unlike the ones reported in this chapter based on the data of both men and women.

Selecting twenty-seven variables, among the very many possible, without being arbitrary was difficult (see Tables XIX and XXXVII, for example). First, a decision was made to refer to the already pared down choices seen in the principal component analyses of Tables XIX and XXXIX. The latter table is composed of twenty-eight task variables and the former of eleven. These thirty-nine variables plus three for age, sex, and education required an elimination of twelve variables to meet the Cattell guideline.

Second, a decision was made to have a representation of the memory/learning variables (Table XXXIX) as equal as possible to the others (Table XIX). There were eleven task variables in Table XIX and all of these were selected; these eleven plus the three subject variables left sixteen to be chosen among the twenty-eight of Table XXXIX.

The sixteen memory/learning variables were selected on the following basis: first those measures with low loadings on the first three factors[3] obtained in the principal component analysis of the memory tasks as reported in Table XXXIX were eliminated,[4] next, five of the span and pattern tasks were eliminated. These had loadings similar to the remaining four span and pattern tasks, but were of a lesser magnitude.[5] Last, one of the measures of long-term memory (the period of 1950-1969) was eliminated for the same reason. The remaining sixteen variables, along with the eleven measures of related functioning, plus the three subject variables may be seen in Tables XL and XLI.

Correlations

The twenty-seven performance scores on tests given to both men and women, and the three subject description variables,

---

[3]It will be recalled that the fourth factor was not psychologically meaningful and contained only one measure with a high loading. Therefore, it was considered of lesser importance.

[4]These included the two measures of delayed memory, the two measures of memory for visual forms, recognition of auditory words, and recognition of meaningful objects.

[5]The tasks eliminated were Auditory Letters Forward, Auditory Letters Backward, Visual Digits Forward, Visual Digits Backward, and Kinesthetic Patterns.

MATRIX OF CORRELATION COEFFICIENTS (r), N = 120:

	1	2	3	4	5	6	7	8	9	10	11	12
1. Age		02	—48	—09	00	—03	—31	—33	—41	—20	—16	—51
2. Sex			03	—40	—41	—46	—05	—04	—09	03	—02	—09
3. Education				29	22	16	17	32	24	12	15	39
4. Long-Term Memory 2					69	65	17	21	03	03	10	27
5. Long-Term Memory 3						62	14	15	02	—03	07	09
6. Long-Term Memory 4							18	11	03	—08	05	14
7. Auditory Digits Forward								47	36	40	10	14
8. Auditory Digits Backward									41	37	23	27
9. Patterns, Auditory										30	11	25
10. Patterns, Visual											01	03
11. Paired Associates 1												33
12. Serial Learning 1												
13. Serial Learning 2												
14. Logical Paragraphs												
15. Silly Paragraphs												
16. Visual Words												
17. Meaningless Objects												
18. Following Instructions 1												
19. Following Instructions 2												
20. VOT (Hooper)												
21. Trailmaking A												
22. Trailmaking B												
23. Copying Digits												
24. Crossing-Off												
25. Slow Writing												
26. Vocabulary												
27. Life Satisfaction												
28. Control Rating												
29. Clinical Impression												
30. Health Rating												

––––––

Note: For all tests high scores represent good performances and low scores represent poor

MEMORY/LEARNING AND RELATED DATA

13	14	15	16	17	18	19	20	21	22	23	24	25	26	27	28	29	30
—52	—42	—53	—44	—39	—43	—49	—59	—46	—42	—62	—63	—39	—27	04	—11	—17	—25
—04	30	18	12	05	—02	—06	24	—02	—11	—07	—06	—39	18	—06	—09	—33	—46
38	24	40	22	29	31	21	38	41	31	51	47	36	49	—05	14	35	28
15	11	06	11	10	06	04	—00	09	11	22	22	23	35	04	03	25	11
09	12	03	—02	05	—06	—01	—10	—01	05	11	15	17	36	04	02	30	01
12	01	—00	05	08	00	05	—01	03	04	13	11	23	26	01	—01	34	—01
26	—02	41	22	13	26	25	07	17	25	35	35	40	26	07	24	24	09
38	18	58	22	30	37	24	25	35	22	42	44	35	33	12	15	30	12
30	16	40	29	26	27	27	27	28	26	46	42	31	17	12	01	09	11
05	02	23	13	07	26	19	11	30	36	28	20	16	16	—03	14	10	10
31	29	28	30	23	15	26	25	05	18	22	19	16	23	—00	13	25	03
54	40	47	41	30	38	40	43	31	20	39	34	23	32	07	14	25	16
	36	54	34	47	47	39	39	24	21	42	37	32	35	06	07	31	16
		47	44	30	23	28	47	27	25	31	24	—04	45	—01	02	—06	15
			39	28	34	27	53	32	24	41	45	32	40	12	13	11	19
				24	27	19	46	26	20	36	30	19	23	—08	02	—01	21
					28	31	42	22	25	30	26	30	43	—03	12	14	18
						46	20	34	39	28	31	31	29	—00	03	24	16
							30	24	34	28	24	30	17	09	16	36	19
								32	24	45	36	18	31	05	05	—05	19
									42	56	41	20	27	—05	10	21	15
										43	32	30	22	08	22	16	23
											77	40	29	02	10	23	20
												39	26	03	06	19	14
													22	—07	11	31	19
														—03	02	15	20
															24	12	17
																16	35
																	11

performances. All coefficients multiplied by 100.

age, sex, and education level, were intercorrelated, providing the matrix seen as Table XL. Coefficients of correlation (r) in this table are statistically significant at less than the .01 level when greater than 0.23 and significant at less than the .05 level when greater than 0.17. Two hundred eighteen of the 435 coefficients were 0.23 or greater.

Components

The data of Table XL were organized by principal component analysis, with the results seen in Table XLI. Four factors were rotated on the basis of the criterion used in Chapters 8 and 16, i.e. on the basis of explained variance of the unrotated factors (see Cattell, 1966; footnote 1 of Chapter 8). The first four factors accounted for 50 percent of the variance.

With rotation, the organizational structure of memory seen in Chapter 16 was seen here again. There were the three memory factors: one was of general short-term memory, another of long-term memory, and one of memory for spans and patterns. The fourth rotated factor was a personality and health factor on which one memory task was represented.

The first factor accounted for 16 percent of the variance after rotation. This general short-term memory factor retained the identity seen in Chapter 16 even with the other, nonmemory tasks which were represented on it. Age ($-.58$) was an important element on this factor and education ($.48$) was somewhat less so. As age increased, performances tended to decline; high education was associated with good short-term memory performance. The memory tasks very prominent here were the two of recall of paragraph sentences (the logical sentences task loaded .79 and the silly .60—see Chapter 12), and the two recall tasks of serial learning (with loadings of .65 and .61). Other short-term memory tasks were also prominent, as may be seen by examining factor 1 of Table XLI.

Two functions, not classed as memory, were important to this short-term memory factor: performance on the Hooper Test of Visual Organization (VOT) and on the WAIS Vocabulary test. As already indicated, the former test, measuring brain function/perception, typically shows decline with age. The

Vocabulary test, measuring an important aspect of intellectual function, tends not to show decline with age. In the present analysis, both were age-related and part of the short-term memory factor.

These results may be seen as paradoxical, especially in view of Tables XIX and XXI, where the memory/learning performances were not examined. In those tables the VOT and Vocabulary test performances were independent, they loaded on different factors. Whether this apparent paradox should be taken as artifact, or whether it should be taken as something more significant requires further research attention.

The second factor accounting for 11 percent of the variance after rotation is all that might have been anticipated from Tables XIX and XXXIX. This factor could be labeled a sex factor, with women appearing to the examiner as less intact clinically than men and being particularly poor in the recall of old information. For some unexplained reason there was an appreciable sex difference (loading of −.63) in regard to the scale rating of Clinical Impression (.47) and performances on the three measures of long-term memory (.82 to .84). This rather strange complex is without reference in the published literature known to us; some speculations, therefore, will be offered shortly.

The third factor accounted for 16 percent of the variance after rotation. This factor of memory ability for spans and patterns was similar to the one identified in Chapter 16 where only memory/learning tasks were examined. Represented highly on this factor were the tasks of auditory digit span forward (.64) and backward (.60), and both auditory and visual patterns (.60 and .65, respectively). Again, performances on these declined with increasing age (−.55). Unlike the principal component analysis based on only the memory/learning data (Table XXXIX), where the age relationship was much the greater with performances associated with the general short-term memory factor than with those of spans and patterns, Table XLI shows that age was equally associated with both factors.

In addition to span and pattern tasks, factor 3 was represented by brain function/perception tasks and by psychomotor speed

TABLE XLI

ROTATED FACTORS OF PRINCIPAL COMPONENT
ANALYSES OF DATA IN TABLE XL

Variable	Factors 1	2	3	4
Subject Description				
1. Age	—.58	.03	—.55	—.11
2. Sex	.32	—.63	—.15	—.21
3. Education	.48	.26	.38	.05
Long-Term Memory				
4. Period: 1930-1949	.17	.82	.06	—.05
5. 1910-1929	.09	.84	—.02	—.07
6. 1890-1909	.07	.83	.01	—.04
Spans and Patterns				
7. Auditory Digits Forward	—.01	.15	.64	.17
8. Auditory Digits Backward	.24	.14	.60	.15
9. Auditory Patterns	.19	—.02	.62	.01
10. Visual Patterns	—.10	—.12	.65	.04
Short-Term Memory				
11. Paired Associates 1	.44	.11	—.01	.28
12. Serial Learning 1	.65	.17	.16	.26
13. Serial Learning 2	.61	.13	.26	.27
Paragraphs				
14. Logical	.79	—.06	—.01	—.06
15. Silly	.60	—.06	.44	.11
Recognition				
16. Visual Words	.58	—.06	.24	—.06
17. Meaningless Objects	.53	.06	.18	.18
Concentration				
18. Following Instructions 1	.33	—.03	.44	.28
19. Following Instructions 2	.34	.00	.29	.51
Brain Function/Perception				
20. VOT (Hooper)	.72	—.18	.22	—.01
21. Trailmaking A	.30	—.01	.57	—.03
22. Trailmaking B	.19	.02	.51	.27
Psychomotor Speed				
23. Copying Digits	.41	.13	.69	—.05
24. Crossing-Off	.36	.15	.66	—.09
25. Slow Writing	.09	.34	.55	.20
Intelligence				
26. Vocabulary	.59	.31	.16	—.06
Personality/Morale				
27. Life Satisfaction	—.02	—.03	—.05	.49
28. Control Rating	—.02	.00	.10	.66
Health/Habit				
29. Clinical Impression	.03	.47	.23	.47
30. Health Rating	.21	.01	.12	.47
Percent Variance	16	11	16	7

tasks. In the former category, there were Trailmaking A and B (loading .57 and .51, respectively); and in the latter category, there were Copying Digits (.69), Crossing-Off (.66) and Slow Writing (.55). The fact, that each of these (except for Slow Writing) requires an ability to respond quickly and that spans and patterns are, by definition, sequential stimuli quickly paced, suggests that this factor is one of ability to process sequential information quickly.

It is to be noted that these results and this interpretation are not exactly the same as those in Chapter 8. Table XIX disclosed a first factor in which the speeded psychomotor tasks loaded with the tasks of brain function/perception, including the VOT (Hooper). This inclusion suggests the interpretation that the speed tasks measure, or are related to, central intactness (see Conclusion section of Chapter 8). The present analysis suggests that, if the speed functions have this character, it might be limited to the quick processing of incoming sequential information. More will be said about this in the Conclusions section of this chapter.

The fourth factor, one of personality and health, accounting for 7 percent of the variance after rotation, is quite independent of age, sex, or education level of the subject. Moreover, with the exception of one memory task (Following Instructions) no cognitive, perceptual, or psychomotor function is represented. This factor indicates that people who see themselves as healthy (Health Rating, .47) tend to be relatively happy (Life Satisfaction, .49) and feel in control of things (Control Rating, .66). For some unexplained reason, this complex, as indicated, was associated with one of the two Following Instruction Task performances.

Whatever the similarity between this personality-health complex and that seen in Table XIX, a major difference resides in the relationship to education level and Vocabulary ability. These two latter variables almost always go together; they were associated with the personality-health complex in Table XIX, but not here (Table XLI). Here, they were associated with short-term memory.

CONCLUSIONS

Memory, like intelligence and many other functions as well, is not a unitary ability; it is a variety of functions and skills. A person may be rated high in one variety and low in another. The present study disclosed three varieties which were roughly described as general short-term memory, memory for spans and patterns, and long-term memory. Increased adult age was associated with relatively poor performances in the first two varieties, but not with the third.

There were two distinctions made between the first two varieties—memory for spans and patterns and general short-term memory. The latter was thought to involve a longer-term holding of information in storage than the former. It was also thought that a need for more complete registration of information in the nervous system might be required in short-term memory than in recall of spans and patterns. The short-term recall was akin to the formulation of secondary memory (SM) of Waugh and Norman (1965) while the recall of spans and patterns was seen as more fleeting, although perhaps not quite as fleeting as primary memory (PM). Accordingly, it seems rather surprising that most of the brain function/perception tasks and related psychomotor speed tasks were associated with the spans and patterns, and not with the more general short-term memory tasks.

An examination of these results stressed the need for a refinement in conceptualizing the relationship between performances of brain function/perception and psychomotor speed. This refinement demanded an analysis of the requirements for successful performance on the spans and patterns tasks.

The memory tasks of spans and patterns have items of information (digits, rhythms) which are presented sequentially by the investigator. The sequential presentations must be fairly rapid or else they will lose their span or pattern character. The subject, therefore, must process these incoming sequences and do it quickly.

The brain function/perception tasks — except the VOT (Hooper)—and the psychomotor speed tasks also have this demand for rapid sequential processing. The two Trailmaking tests (A and B) and the two speeded psychomotor tests (Copying Digits and Crossing-Off) are each made up of a single sheet of paper with items of information on it. The subject moves on from one item to the next as he completes them; the more quickly he works, the more rapid the functional sequencing of incoming information. Thus, the spans and patterns tasks, these brain function/perception tasks, and the psychomotor speed tasks, all require sequential processing.

Not all speed tasks, it would seem, have this character. For example, simple reaction time tasks do not have them and thus would not be expected to show this pattern. This formulation, in fact, was supported in a recent study which disclosed only a small correlation between reaction time and performances on the two speeded psychomotor tasks of the present study (Botwinick and Storandt, 1973). Performances on the speed tasks of this study, those requiring sequential processing of information, may be conceived as an aspect of brain function/perception. But, as such, it is a special circumscribed aspect, not general to all aspects of brain function/perception.

A different aspect of brain function/perception may be seen by the factor on which both short-term memory and VOT (Hooper) performances were represented. This memory—a type thought more dependent upon registration, storage, and retrieval mechanisms—is associated more with brain function measured by the VOT than the sequential processing tasks, Trailmaking and psychomotor speed. The VOT measures an ability to organize in mind, to make into a unified whole, spatially disparate parts of objects. This mental skill, it seems, is helpful, or at least related to ability in short-term recall.

Thus the two different types of memory are each associated with a different aspect of brain function/perception: memory for spans and patterns is associated with sequential processing of information, and short-term memory is associated with mental organization regarding spatial relations. Increasing adult age was seen associated with poorer performances on both types of memory and both types of associated brain function/perception tasks.

The second factor bearing on yet a different type of memory, long-term memory, was a most interesting one. It could be labeled as a sex factor, showing that women performed relatively poorly in long-term recall and gave the impression of being less adequate in a mental health sense than men. It is well known that women are no more sick physically than men and that women outlive men. Why do they appear less well otherwise? Two possible answers come to mind. One, women, especially middle-aged and older women, may be more comfortable than men in showing or expressing weakness. Social roles seem to allow women—if not demand of them—such signs of fallability. Men must be strong and stoic, even to the end perhaps. Two, another possible explanation of the apparent sex difference in mental health is that the women were in fact poorer than men. Most of the subjects were middle-aged (the total age range was from twenty to seventy-nine years). Perhaps the middle age is more difficult for women than men, it is the age when children leave home, when menopause starts, when one's youth is recently gone. For men, such experience may be of much less trauma than for women.

Women rated as being in relatively poor mental health performed poorly on tasks of long-term memory. Why long-term memory? It was explained in Chapter 16 that the long-term memory tasks were developed with the assumption that the information tested was at one time equally known to all comparison groups. It may well be that in regard to the comparison of men and women, this assumption was not correct. It may well be that different educational opportunities, different demands and expectations have developed woman much less informed about the world than man. Future comparisons in the long-term recall of information may show a greater equality between men and woman.

While women were seen by the investigators as being of poorer mental health than men, they did not seem to be less happy or feel less in control of the life around them (factor 2). Those, however, who rated themselves as not very healthy physically, men and women both, tended to be less happy and feel less in control. The fourth rotated factor suggested this complex. Those men and women less healthy, happy, and not in control were also seen by the investigator as being in relatively poor mental health. This complex was as true for the old as for the young. Health, and not age, therefore, was the focal point of feelings of well being.

REFERENCES

Arenberg, D.: Anticipation interval and age differences in verbal learning. *J Abnorm Psychol,* 70:419-425, 1965.

Bartko, J. J.; Patterson, R. D., and Butler, R. N.: Biomedical and behavioral predictors of survival among normal aged men: a multivariate analysis. In Palmore, E., and Jeffers, F. C. (Eds.): *Prediction of Life Span.* Lexington, Mass., Heath, 1971, pp. 123-137.

Battersby, W. S.; Krieger, N. P.; Pollack, M., and Bender, M. B.: Figure-ground discrimination and the "abstract attitude" in patients with cerebral neo-plasma. *Archives of Neurology and Psychiatry,* 70:703-712, 1953.

Birren, J. E.: *The Psychology of Aging.* Englewood Cliffs, N.J., Prentice Hall, 1964.

Birren, J. E., and Botwinick, J.: The relation of writing speed to age and to the senile psychoses. *J Consult Psychol,* 15:243-249, 1951.

Birren, J. E.; Butler, R. N.; Greenhouse, S. W.; Sokoloff, L., and Yarrow, M. R.: *Human Aging.* Washington, D.C., U.S. Government Printing Office, 1963.

Birren, J. E., and Morrison, D. F.: Analysis of the WAIS subtests in relation to age and education. *J Gerontol,* 16:363-369, 1961.

Bock, R. D.: Programming univariate and multivariate analysis of variance. *Technometrics,* 5:95-117, 1963.

Bock, R. D.: Contributions of multivariate experimental designs to educational research. In Cattell, R. B. (Ed.): *Handbook of Multivariate Experimental Psychology.* Chicago, Rand, 1966, pp. 820-840.

Bock, R. D., and Haggard, E. A.: The use of multivariate analysis of variance in behavioral research. In Dean Whitla (Ed.): *Handbook of Measurement in Education, Psychology, and Sociology.* Boston, Addison Wesley, 1968, pp. 100-142.

Bortner, R. W., and Hultsch, D. F.: A multivariate analysis of correlates of life satisfaction in adulthood. *J Gerontol,* 25:41-47, 1970.

Botwinick, J.: Drives, expectancies, and emotions. In J. E. Birren (Ed.): *Handbook of Aging and the Individual.* Chicago, U of Chicago Pr, 1959, pp. 739-768.

Botwinick, J.: Theories of antecedent conditions of speed of response. In Welford, A. T., and Birren, J. E. (Eds.): *Behavior, Aging and the Nervous System.* Springfield, Thomas, 1965, pp. 67-87.

Botwinick, J.: *Cognitive Processes in Maturity and Old Age.* New York, Springer Pub, 1967.

Botwinick, J.: *Aging and Behavior*. New York, Springer Pub, 1973.

Botwinick, J.; Brinley, J. F., and Robbin, J. S.: Modulation of speed of response with age. *J Genet Psychol*, 95:137-144, 1959.

Botwinick, J., and Storandt, M.: Speed functions, vocabulary, and age. *Percept Mot Skills*, 36:1123-1128, 1973.

Botwinick, J., and Thompson, L. W.: Depressive affect, speed of response, and age. *J Consult Psychol*, 31:106, 1967.

Broadbent, D. E.: *Perception and Communication*. New York, Pergamon, 1958.

Brodman, K.; Erdmann, A. J., Jr.; Lorge, I., and Wolff, H. G.: The Cornell Medical Index—Health Questionnaire: VI. The relation of patients' complaints to age, sex, race and education. *J Gerontol*, 8:339-342, 1953.

Brodman, K.; Erdmann, A. J., Jr., and Wolff, H. G.: *Cornell Medical Index Health Questionnaire*. New York, Cornell Medical College, 1949.

Bromley, D. B.: Some effects of age on short-term learning and remembering. *J Gerontol*, 13:398-406, 1958.

Canestrari, R. E., Jr.: Paced and self-paced learning in young and elderly adults. *J Gerontol*, 18:165-168, 1963.

Cattell, R. B.: *Factor Analysis: An Introduction and Manual for the Psychologist and Social Scientist*. New York, Harper and Row, 1952.

Cattell, R. B.: The scree test for the number of factors. *Multivariate Behavioral Research*, 1:245-276, 1966.

Cattell, R. B.; Eber, H. W., and Tatsuoka, M. M.: *Handbook for Sixteen Personality Factor Questionnaire*. Champaign, Ill., Institute for Personality and Ability Testing, 1970.

Davis, S. H., and Obrist, W. D.: Age differences in learning and retention of verbal material. *Cornell Journal of Social Relations*, 1:95-103, 1966.

Eisdorfer, C.: Verbal learning and response time in the aged. *J Genet Psychol*, 107:15-22, 1965.

Eisdorfer, C.; Axelrod, S., and Wilkie, F.: Stimulus exposure time as a factor in serial learning in an aged sample. *J Abnorm Soc Psychol*, 67:594-600, 1963.

Erber, J. T.: Age differences in recognition memory. *J Gerontol*, 29:177-181, 1974.

Fozard, J. L.: Predicting age in the adult years from psychological assessments of abilities and personality. *Aging and Human Development*, 3:175-182, 1972.

Fozard, J. L., and Nuttall, R. L.: Effects of age and socioeconomic status differences on the sixteen personality factor questionnaire scores. *Proceedings, 79th Annual Convention, APA*, 1971, pp. 597-598.

Fozard, J. L., and Waugh, N. C.: Proactive inhibition of prompted items. *Psychonomic Science*, 17:67-68, 1969.

Garrity, T., and Klein, R. F.: A behavioral predictor of survival among heart attack patients. In Palmore, E., and Jeffers, F. C. (Eds.): *Prediction of Life Span*. Lexington, Mass, Heath, 1971, pp. 215-222.

Gilbert, J. G.: Memory loss in senescence. *J Abnorm Soc Psychol, 36*:73-86, 1941.

Goodwin, K. S., and Schaie, K. W.: Age differences in personality structure. *Proceedings, 77th Annual Convention, APA, 4*:713-714, 1969.

Hathaway, S. R., and McKinley, J. C.: Scale 2 (Depression). In Welsh, G. S., and Dahlstrom, W. G. (Eds.): *Basic Readings on the MMPI in Psychology and Medicine.* Minneapolis, U of Minn Pr, 1956, pp. 73-80.

Hays, W. L.: *Statistics.* New York, HR&W, 1963.

Hicks, L. H., and Birren, J. E.: Aging, brain damage and psychomotor slowing. *Psychol Bull, 74*:377-396, 1970.

Hollingshead, A. B.: *Two-factor Index of Social Position,* 1957. (Mimeo.)

Hooper, H. E.: *The Hooper Visual Organization Test—Manual.* Beverly Hills, Psychological Services, 1958.

Hulicka, I. M.: Age differences in retention as a function of interference. *J Gerontol, 22*:180-184, 1967.

Hulicka, I. M., and Weiss, R. L.: Age differences in retention as a function of learning. *J Consult Psychol, 29*:125-129, 1965.

Jerome, E. A.: Age and learning—experimental studies. In Birren, J. E. (Ed.): *Handbook of Aging and the Individual: Psychological and Biological Aspects.* Chicago. U of Chicago Pr, 1959, pp. 655-699.

Jones, H. E., and Kaplan, D. J.: Psychological aspects of mental disorders in late life. In Kaplan, O. J. (Ed.): *Mental Disorders in Later Life, 2nd ed.* Stanford, Stanford U Pr, 1956, pp. 98-156.

Kaiser, H. F.: The application of electronic computers to factor analysis. *Educational and Psychological Measurement, 20*:141-151, 1960.

Kapnick, P.: *Age and Recognition Memory.* Unpublished dissertation, Washington University, 1971.

Kay, H.: Learning and aging. In Schaie, K. W. (Ed.): *Theory and Methods of Research on Aging.* Morgantown, WVa U Pr, 1968, pp .61-82.

Kilpatrick, F. P., and Cantril, H.: Self-anchoring scaling: A measure of individuals' unique reality worlds. *J Individ Psychol, 16*:158-173, 1960.

Kinsbourne, M.: Age effects on letter span related to rate and sequential dependency. *J Gerontol, 28*:317-319, 1973.

Maddox, G. L., and Eisdorfer, C.: Some correlates of activity and morale among the elderly. *Social Forces, 40*:254-260, 1962.

McGhie, A.; Chapman, W., and Lawson, J. S.: Changes in immediate memory with age. *Br J Psychol, 56*:69-75, 1965.

Melton, A. W.: Implications of short-term memory for a general theory of memory. *Journal of Verbal Learning and Verbal Behavior, 2*:1-21, 1963.

Moenster, P. A.: Learning and memory in relation to age. *J Gerontol, 27*:361-363, 1972.

Monge, R. H., and Hultsch, D.: Paired-associate learning as a function of adult age and the length of the anticipation and inspection intervals. *J Gerontol, 26*:157-162, 1971.

Neugarten, B. L.; Crotty, W. F., and Tobin, S. S.: *Personality in Middle and Late Life.* New York, Atherton, 1964.

Neugarten, B. L., and Gutmann, D. L.: Age-sex roles and personality in middle age: A thematic apperception study. *Psychol Monogr, 72:* No. 17, Whole No. 470, 1958.

Neugarten, B. L.; Havighurst, R. J., and Tobin, S. S.: Personality and patterns of aging. In Neugarten, B. L. (Ed.): *Middle Age and Aging.* Chicago, U of Chicago Pr, 1968, pp. 173-177.

Overall, J. E., and Spiegel, D. K.: Concerning least squares analyses of experimental data. *Psychol Bull, 72*:311-322, 1969.

Perlin, S., and Butler, R. N.: Psychiatric aspects of adaptation to the aging experience. In Birren, J. E., et al. (Eds.): *Human Aging.* Washington, D.C., U.S. Government Printing Office, 1963, pp. 159-213.

Reed, H. B. C., Jr., and Reitan, R. M.: Changes in psychological test performance associated with the normal aging process. *J Gerontol, 18*:271-274, 1963.

Ross, J. E.: Simplification of human abilities with age in four social class groups. *Proceedings, 78th Annual Convention, APA,* 1970, pp. 685-686.

Rummel, R. J.: *Applied Factor Analysis.* Evanston, Northwestern U Pr, 1970.

Schaie, K. W.: Age changes and age differences. *Gerontologist, 7*:128-132, 1967.

Schonfield, D.: Memory changes with age. *Nature, 28*:918, 1965.

Schonfield, D., and Robertson, B.: Memory storage and aging. *Can J Psychol, 20*:228-236, 1966.

Schonfield, D.; Trueman, V., afd Kline, D.: Recognition tests of dichotic listening and the age variable. *J Gerontol, 27*:487-493, 1972.

Shakow, D.; Dolkart, M. B., and Goldman, R.: The memory function in psychoses of the aged. *Dis Nerv Syst, 2*:43-48, 1941.

Sperling, G.: The information available in brief visual presentations. *Psychol Monogr, 74:* No. 11, 1-28, 1960.

Talland, G. A.: Age and span of immediate recall. In Talland, G. A. (Ed.): *Human Aging and Behavior.* New York, Acad Pr, 1968, pp. 93-129.

Taub, H. A.: Memory span, practice, and aging. *J Gerontol, 28*:335-338, 1973.

Teuber, H. L.; Battersby, W. S., and Bender, M. B.: Performance of complex visual tasks after cerebral lesions. *J Nerv Ment Dis, 114*:413-429, 1951.

Thurstone, L. L.: *A Factorial Study of Perception.* Chicago. U of Chicago Pr, 1944.

Tulving, E., and Thomson, D. M.: Retrieval processes in recognition memory: Effects of associative context. *Journal of Verbal Learning and Verbal Behavior, 87*:116-124, 1971.

U.S. Bureau of Census: *Census of Population, 1970. Detailed Characteristics. Final Report* PC (1)-D1. United States Summary. Washington, D.C., U.S. Government Printing Office, 1973, p. 628.

U.S. Public Health Service: *Smoking and Health.* Report of the Advisory Committee to the Surgeon General. Washington, D.C., U.S. Government Printing Office, Publication No. 1103, 1964.

U.S. Public Health Service: *Monthly Vital Statistic Report, 18*: No. 13, 1970. Table G, p. 6-7. Washington, D.C., U.S. Government Printing Office.

Waugh, N. C., and Norman, D. A.: Primary memory. *Psychol Rev, 72*:89-104, 1965.

Wechsler, D.: *Manual for the Wechsler Adult Intelligence Scale.* New York, The Psychological Corporation, 1955.

Wechsler, D.: *The Measurement and Appraisal of Adult Intelligence.* Baltimore, Williams & Wilkins, 1958.

Wechsler, D.: Intelligence, memory and the aging process. In Hock, P. H., and Zubin, J. (Eds.): *Psychopathology of Aging.* New York, Grune, 1961, pp. 152-159.

THE TESTS IN THE ORDER IN WHICH THEY WERE ADMINISTERED

FIRST, THE MEMORY/LEARNING tasks (Part II of this book) were given, then the other age-related tasks (Part I).

TASKS OF PART II

1. Visual Word Recognition
2. Auditory Word Recognition
3. Auditory Digits Forward
4. Auditory Digits Backward
5. Paired Associates 1
6. Paired Associates 2
7. Recognizable Visual Forms 1
8. Visual Patterns
9. Auditory Patterns
10. Kinesthetic Patterns
11. Paired Associates 1 Delayed Recall
12. Paired Associates 2 Delayed Recall
13. Auditory Letters Forward
14. Auditory Letters Backward
15. Serial Learning 1
16. Following Instructions 1
17. Following Instructions 2
18. Serial Learning 1 Delayed Recall
19. Visual Digits Forward
20. Visual Digits Backward
21. Paired Associates 3
22. Meaningful Object Recognition

23. Meaningless Object Recognition
24. Meaningless Visual Forms
25. Paired Associates 3 Delayed Recall
26. Logical Paragraphs
27. Serial Learning 2
28. Auditory Digits Forward with Interference
29. Auditory Digits Backward with Interference
30. Silly Paragraphs
31. Long-Term Memory 1950-1969
32. Long-Term Memory 1930-1949
33. Long-Term Memory 1910-1929
34. Long-Term Memory 1890-1909

TASKS OF PART I

1. Copying Digits
2. Crossing-Off
3. Slow Writing
4. Trailmaking A
5. Trailmaking B
*6. WAIS Comprehension
7. WAIS Vocabulary
*8. WAIS Block Design
*9. WAIS Picture Arrangement
10. Health Rating
11. Control Rating
12. Life Satisfaction Rating
*13. Embedded Figures
*14. MMPI D-scale
15. Hooper Visual Organization Test (VOT)
*16. Cornell Medical Index
*17. 16 PF

------

*These tasks were not administered to male subjects.

APPENDIX B

PROCEDURES OF AGE-RELATED
BEHAVIOR TASKS (PART I)

C HAPTERS 3 THROUGH 7 were of behaviors other than memory/ learning. In these chapters of Part I, the procedures used either were described in the text or could be seen in the published literature. There were two exceptions, both in Chapter 7 (Health and Health Habits): the Clinical Impression Scale and the Habits Questionnaire—both developed here for the present purposes. Scores on the questionnaire are based on information given by the subject; ratings on the scale are based solely on impressions of the examiner about the subject.

CLINICAL IMPRESSION SCALE

1. Does S appear to be in good contact?   Yes....*.. No........
2. Was rapport good?   Yes....*.. No........
3. Was S anxious?   Yes........ No....*..
4. Would you say S has seen better days recently?   Yes........ No....*..
5. Did S have difficulty understanding instructions?   Yes........ No....*..
6. Did S appear physically robust as compared to physically frail?   Yes....*.. No........
7. Did you like the S?   Yes....*.. No........
8. Did you feel uncomfortable with the S?   Yes........ No....*..
9. Did you feel you had to be gentle and supportive with the S?   Yes........ No....*..
10. Did S appear to or try to "make conversation" as compared to responding only to direct questions?   Yes....*.. No........
11. Did S appear to be able to see well?   Yes....*.. No........
12. Was S neat and well-kempt in appearance?   Yes....* No........
13. Did S exhibit any instances of bizarre thought processes?   Yes........ No....*..
14. Did S appear depressed?   Yes........ No....*..
15. Was S angry?   Yes........ No....*..
16. Did S cry?   Yes........ No....*..
17. Was S concerned about his failures?   Yes........ No....*..

18. Did S make disparaging comments about the test
    or examiner?   Yes......... No....*..
19. Did S make any attempt to terminate testing before
    completion?   Yes......... No....*..
20. Did S appear ego-involved in the tasks?   Yes....*.. No.........
21. Did you feel sorry for the S?   Yes......... No....*..
22. Did S look like he was in "bad shape?"   Yes......... No....*..

――――――

*Responses scored in a positive direction indicated by asterisks.

HABITS QUESTIONNAIRE

1. How old are you?........................
2. Have you ever smoked? Regularly (daily)   Occasionally   No
   (If no, skip to No. 10.)
3. How old were you when you began smoking?........................
4. Do you smoke now?   Regularly (daily)   Occasionally   No
5. If no, how old were you when you stopped smoking?........................
6. What do (did) you smoke?   Cigarettes   Pipe   Cigars
7. How much do (did) you smoke?
       Cigarettes (number per day)....................
       Pipe (number ounces per week)....................
       Cigars (number per week)....................
8. Do (did) you inhale?
       Cigarettes   Yes   No
       Pipe   Yes   No
       Cigars   Yes   No
9. Rate the amount you smoke (smoked)   Heavy   Medium   Light
10. Have you ever used alcoholic beverages?   Yes   No
    (If no, terminate questionnaire.)
11. How old were you when you began drinking?........................
12. Do you drink now?   Yes   No
13. If no, how old were you when you stopped drinking?........................
14. What do (did) you drink?   Beer   Liquor   Wine
15. How much do (did) you drink?

	Ounces per week	Ounces per month
Beer	....	....
Liquor	....	....
Wine	....	....

16. Rate the amount you drink.   Little   Moderate   Heavy

APPENDIX C

PROCEDURES OF MEMORY/LEARNING TASKS (PART II)

C HAPTERS 9 THROUGH 15 were of the memory/learning investigations. In four of these seven chapters constituting Part II of this book, the procedures were described fully, or in detail sufficient to make them clear. In three chapters, however, the procedures were not so described; they are Chapters 9, 14 and 15, the procedures of which are described below.

LONG-TERM MEMORY (CHAPTER 9)

Twenty-four long-term memory questions were asked each subject, six in each of four time periods. These are the questions, with the correct answers in parentheses.

Period: 1950-1969

1. What was the name of the first man to set foot on the moon? (Neil Armstrong)
2. What was the name of the man who assassinated Dr. Martin Luther King? (James Earl Ray)
3. In what city was President John F. Kennedy assassinated? (Dallas)
4. In what year did the Russians orbit the first satellite? (1957)
5. What was the name of the man who ran against Dwight Eisenhower for President in 1952 and again in 1956? (Adlai Stevenson)
6. What was the name of the Senator from Wisconsin whose name is associated with congressional investigations of communism in the early 1950's? (Joseph McCarthy)

Period: 1930-1949

7. What was the name of the man who was elected vice-president in 1948 when Harry Truman was elected president? (Alvin Barkley)

8. What was the name of the World War II German general nicknamed "The Desert Fox?" (Erwin Rommel)

9. What was the name of the commander of the famous Flying Tigers of World War II? (Claire Chenault)

10. On what date (day, month, year) did the Japanese bomb Pearl Harbor? (December 7, 1941)

11. What was the name of the only president of the United States to be elected to four terms of office? (Franklin Roosevelt)

12. Where (in what state) did the German dirigible, the Von Hindenberg, burn and crash? (New Jersey)

Period: 1910-1929

13. What was the name of the ship which hit an iceberg and sank on its maiden voyage in 1912? (Titanic)

14. What was the name of the man whose death set off World War I? (Archduke Ferdinand)

15. What was the name of the World War I German flying ace nicknamed "The Red Baron?" (Baron Manfred Von Richtohfen)

16. What do the initials WCTU stand for? (Women's Christian Temperance Union)

17. What was the name of the man tried in the famous Monkey Trial of 1925? (John T. Scopes)

18. What was the name of the plane in which Lindbergh flew the Atlantic? (Spirit of St. Louis)

Period: 1890-1909

19. What was the name of the man who discovered the North Pole? (Robert E. Peary)

20. In what state did the first legal electrocution for murder in the United States occur? (New York)

21. What was the name of the man who became president when President McKinley was assassinated in 1900? (Theodore Roosevelt)

22. Where did the Wright brothers make their first successful flight? (Kitty Hawk)
23. What was the name of the boxer who was nicknamed "Gentleman Jim?" (James Corbett)
24. In what year did Henry Ford introduce the Model T? (1908)

RECOGNITION MEMORY (CHAPTER 14)

There were four tasks of recognition memory. Two were of verbal materials and two were of nonverbal. The latter two were described in full in the text. Only the two verbal recognition tasks are presented here.

One of the two verbal tasks involved two lists of words, each presented visually; the other task involved two lists, each presented orally. There were eight words in each of the four lists.

The subject's task was to identify the eight words in a visual display of thirty-two words. The eight words of each list were given in the text. Here, the four displays of thirty-two words each are presented. The subject was shown the thirty-two words in two columns of sixteen words each. Here, to save space, the thirty-two words are given in lists of four each.

Visual Stimuli, List 1

Tail	Chance	Top	Pie	Sea	Law	Prince	Bank
Heart	Net	Yard	World	Train	Hole	School	Noise
Path	Mill	Throat	Sight	Height	Branch	Egg	Map
Voice	Friend	Fish	Range	Growth	Cent	Plate	Boy

Visual Stimuli, List 2

North	Cloud	Thing	Day	Maid	Glass	Nut	Loss
Wit	Board	Wheat	Debt	Health	End	Doctor	Youth
Boat	Shape	Target	Hill	Bridge	Flower	Seat	Man
Ice	Group	Wood	Course	Deck	Street	Pan	Log

Auditory Stimuli, List 1

Side	Country	Wealth	Speech	Lip	Knife	Room	Queen
Time	Bed	Store	Crowd	Gun	Infant	Pound	Person
Front	Valley	Ray	Wall	Next	Buzzer	Eye	Mat
Wheel	Sun	Death	Finger	Cost	Part	Face	Air

Auditory Stimuli, List 2

Number	Bay	Pole	Task	Figure	Neck	Milk	Circle
Tea	Car	Lot	Ear	Coal	Hat	Troop	Guest
Sound	Worker	Worth	Strike	Porch	Dark	Month	Job
Matter	Child	Blood	Parent	Wire	Help	Field	Key

CONCENTRATION AND INTERFERENCE (CHAPTER 15)

Two tasks of Following Instructions were given, one referred to as noninterfering and the other as interfering. These references were suggested by the nature of the instructions.

Each of these two tasks was given in five different levels of difficulty; each task difficulty level was given twice. The level of task difficulty was defined by the number of elements in the task instruction.

Noninterfering

LEVEL I.—1) Put a 1 in the circle. 2)Put a 3 in the square.

LEVEL II.—1) Put a 2 in the square and a 3 in the triangle. 2) Put a 2 in the circle and a 1 in the square.

LEVEL III.—1) Put a 1 in the circle, a 3 in the square, and a 2 in the circle. 2) Put a 3 in the triangle, a 1 in the square, and a 2 in the square.

LEVEL IV.—1) Put a 2 in the square, a 3 in the triangle, a 1 in the triangle, and a 2 in the circle. 2) Put a 1 in the circle, a 2 in the triangle, a 3 in the circle and a 1 in the square.

LEVEL V.—1) Put a 2 in the triangle, a 1 in the circle, a 1 in the triangle, a 3 in the square, and a 3 in the circle. 2) Put a 3 in the square, a 2 in the circle, a 1 in the triangle, a 2 in the square, and a 1 in the triangle.

Interfering

LEVEL I.—1) Make a small square in the triangle. 2) Make a small circle in the square.

LEVEL II.—1) Make a triangle in the square and a circle in the circle. 2) Make a circle in the triangle and a triangle in the circle.

LEVEL III.—1) Make a triangle in the square, a square in the circle, and a circle in the square. 2) Make a square in the triangle, a circle in the square, and a triangle in the triangle.

LEVEL IV.—1) Make a circle in the square, a square in the circle, a square in the triangle, and a triangle in the square. 2) Make a square in the triangle, a circle in the square, a square in the triangle, and a triangle in the circle.

LEVEL V.—1) Make a circle in the square, a square in the circle, a triangle in the square, a square in the triangle, and a triangle in the circle. 2) Make a square in the triangle, a triangle in the square, a circle in the triangle, a circle in the square, and a triangle in the circle.

INDEX